BACK TO THE CABIN

BACK TO THE CABIN

more inspiration for the classic american getaway

DALE MULFINGER author of *The Cabin* | photographs by CHERYL KORALIK

The Taunton Press

The Taunton Press
Inspiration for hands-on living®

The Taunton Press, Inc.
63 South Main Street
PO Box 5506
Newtown, CT 06470-5506
e-mail: tp@taunton.com

EDITOR: Pam Hoenig
COPY EDITOR: Seth Reichgott
INDEXER: Jay Kreider
DESIGN AND LAYOUT: carol singer | notice design
ILLUSTRATOR: Christine Erikson
PHOTOGRAPHER: Cheryl Koralik, except as noted on pp. 248–249

The following name/manufacturer appearing in *Back to the Cabin* is a trademark: Styrofoam®

LIBRARY OF CONGRESS CATALOGING-IN-PUBLICATION DATA
Mulfinger, Dale, 1943-
  Back to the cabin : more inspiration for the classic American getaway / Dale Mulfinger.
     pages cm
  ISBN 978-1-60085-521-4
1. Vacation homes--United States--Design and construction. 2. Log cabins--United States-
-Design and construction. I. Title.
  TH4835.M84 2013
  728.7'2--dc23
                            2013007533

PRINTED IN SINGAPORE
10 9 8 7 6 5 4 3 2 1

ACKNOWLEDGMENTS

Architecture found me in the fall of 1963 as I entered my first architectural design studio at the University of Minnesota. Four years later I graduated with the Class of '67, the greatest group of colleagues I could ever imagine. They have remained my colleagues over these ever so many years, and for all they've taught me and the friendship they've bestowed, I dedicate this book to them.

My special thanks goes out to Peter Chapman and the team he has assembled at The Taunton Press to muster this book through its assemblage: Alison Wilkes, Erin Giunta, Pam Hoenig, Carol Singer, and Seth Reichgott all who tried their best to make me look beyond my best. And kudos to my "new best friend," photographer Cheryl Koralik, for capturing the beauty and poignancy of these very special places.

This book, of course, would not be but for the amazing commitment of owners, architects, interior designers, builders, and a host of craftspeople who invest themselves into meaningful places. My thanks to them all.

And more than thanks to my patient wife, Jan, who bears with me on my unending cabin quest and knows the true meaning of, "Wow, look at that amazing cabin. Can we stop for a minute?"

TABLE OF CONTENTS

Introduction: Getting Away from It All   2

MEMORIES OF YESTERYEAR   10

LUNDIE'S LEGACY   12
PARKS AND REC REDO   20
HER DREAM/HIS ENCHANTMENT   26
BARN LIFE   32
ADIRONDACK CAMP   38
BIRD'S EYE   44
BACKYARD HIDEAWAY   50

ADD AND UPGRADE   56

SING ALONG   58
ADDING CHARM   66
ACCESS TO WATER   72
SIMPLE ELEGANCE   78
"A" PLUS   86
OLD GLORY   92
SUBTRACT AND ADD   98

PREPACKAGED AND GIFT-WRAPPED   104

INSTANT CABIN   106
GEORGIA PEACH   112
THE WELL-CONTAIN(ER)ED CABIN   118
HOME RUN   124
THE HAMLET   130
A KERNEL IDEA   136

STEP LIGHTLY ON THE EARTH 142

STORY LINE 144
ENERGY SHED 150
EARTH AND SKY 156
CABIN CLASSROOM 162
THINKING LOCALLY 168
OPPOSITES ATTRACT 174

JUST FOR THE FUN OF IT 182

BASE CAMP FOR FUN 184
WE TOOK TO THE WOODS 190
A WORK IN PROGRESS 196
ELFIN HEAVEN 202
BOARDING HOUSE 210

LIGHT AND AIR 216

ONE BIG ROOM 218
PANORAMIC VIEW 224
LIGHT SHEDS 230
SCREEN PLAY 236
PORCH WRAP 242

Credits 248

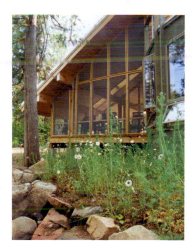

The cabin is tucked into a ledge rock with entry on the second floor. The lake view is to the south.

I go to the cabin to be outdoors, to bond with nature, to have quality time with family and friends, and to dabble in building things. I feed the deer and the birds and make crepes for my grandchildren. I repair my boats and occasionally can keep a motor running long enough to make my way down

GETTING AWAY FROM IT ALL

to the other end of our 23-mile lake for a beer and burger. Or I will putter out to a favorite nearby bay for some fishing, return with a dozen bluegills, and spend an hour cleaning them for dinner.

I may consume the better part of a morning teaching myself (again) how to replace the chain on my chainsaw. I will walk down the hill to the shore to cut up a basswood the beaver has felled only to find I have put the new chain on backward. By dusk I will be exhausted from 30 trips up and down the 28 steps to the lake with 40-pound pieces of tree trunk on my shoulder.

The living and dining areas are delineated by a fieldstone-wrapped fireplace unit capped with fir that is open on both sides. The walls and ceiling are sheathed in pine; the beams are recycled fir. The radiant-heated floor is finished with Vermont slate that was bought at a big box store.

I will read a book, or an article from an outdated *Atlantic* magazine, or the local small-town newspaper. Maybe I'll attack a moderately difficult Sudoku puzzle or challenge my grandson to a vicious checkers match, trying to prove I can still beat him.

I am a bit of a pyromaniac, and I always burn wood at the cabin. In the winter I keep the fireplace burning through the night. During the summer I might get a blaze going in the fire pit and cook some late-night s'mores.

If the lake has warmed for the summer season, a swim might be in order. With a grandchild I will race a few hundred yards to the point and know from my heavy breathing that next year she is sure to win. A spring walk might feature a huge flock of migrating songbirds catching their breath and refueling for their trek into Canada. In the fall season I will enjoy the crunch of fallen birch and aspen leaves beneath my feet as I stroll down our country lane. And in winter varmint tracks may point the way to a fox den.

I occasionally enjoy a long weekend at the cabin in solitude. That's when you can sneak in a few hours just daydreaming and staring into space with no guilt about the time elapsed doing absolutely nothing. But truth be told, I prefer family or a few friends around me, to catch up on the latest tales, to sort through the political turmoil of the month, and to break bread and uncork a bottle of St. Pepin wine.

So why do I have a cabin?

For certain, a few of the experiences I mentioned above also take place at my home in the city. There, too, I can kindle the crackling flame and join family and friends for fine food and good conversation. But many of the other experiences, particularly those having to do with nature, are more difficult to come by and certainly not as serendipitous or spectacular.

No ominous eagle shadow will flit across the city sidewalk, nor call of the loon rise above the distant freeway din.

So why not a tent?

I tried a tent at state parks for a few years, occasionally motorcycling off with my young daughter in tow. An early morning storm and not the best tent placement made for the soggy awakening that tenting and I were not necessarily a match made in heaven. Plus my daughter was growing and, with the larger tent, we would no longer fit on the Honda cycle. My wife and older daughter were also questioning the fairness quotient, although their idea of roughing it includes a bathroom.

Thus was born Le Porch (featured in *The Cabin*, pp. 166–171), my answer to camping without a tent. Located just an hour from our home, our delightful fresh-air structure kept us dry, stored our meager belongings, and gave us space to entertain our friends. But this structure was a one-season dwelling, and although I could put up with a chilly run to the outhouse, after a decade I could see my family was waning in enthusiasm. As I stood in the icy lake late one fall day, taking the dock in and knowing my porch would not warm up my frozen limbs, I considered alternatives.

I could have a cabin farther away, in the wilderness, built to accommodate family and a few friends, one with a warm fireplace and inhabitable for all seasons. I would need the initiative to find the land, the imagination to envision the structure, and perhaps a financial partner to defray the cost.

Lake Vermilion in Northern Minnesota was a place my family had repeatedly returned to over the past few decades. I regularly looked at and reviewed real estate at the lake with resort owner and realtor friend, Mark Ludlow. We would assess property and cabins to find opportunities for improvement and resale. On one occasion Mark discovered a parcel with an old log cabin on it and was contemplating purchasing it for himself. After a site inspection, I informed him that this parcel seemed inappropriate for the Ludlow family but would be a perfect fit for the Mulfinger gang.

The property had character, with a rich variety of red pine, spruce, birch, and poplar trees. Rock outcroppings were prevalent, and a square log cabin sat on a ridge overlooking a quiet bay. A new dock was needed but a natural site already existed at the water's edge for a couple of Adirondack chairs to overlook the beach.

A modest office is built into a balcony off the second-floor bedroom. The walls, floor, and ceiling are all finished in pine of variable widths.

We purchased the property with good friends of ours, the Dittmars. We knew of other couples that had successfully shared a retreat property and we liked the thought of paying only half of the cost. With that additional financial input, we could put on an addition and swap the outhouse for a proper bathroom, which would require putting in a new well and a septic system.

The first summer we used the small cabin without making any changes in order to take stock of what we had. An aluminum fishing boat, a 20-horsepower engine, and considerable ice-fishing equipment were thrown in with the purchase price of the property, as were the appliances, beds, linens, dishes, pots, and pans. Some cleaning and a fresh coat of interior paint were in order, along with the construction

of a dock and stairway to the beach. The outbuildings—a workshop, woodshed, and outhouse—were cleaned and put to use.

After a summer of lake life we were ready to design our future. Our co-owners, Gunter, a university architecture professor, and Susie, a dental hygienist instructor, would weigh in along with my wife, Jan, on the program and design. I was appointed to be the taskmaster, to keep the project flowing so that by the third summer our new digs would be ready for habitation. We collectively set a budget and since I had the experience of getting cabins built nearby, I took on the roles of estimator and sheriff of the budget, with all the responsibilities that come with that.

LEFT Twin ash posts that were provided by timber framer Deane Hillbrand flank the kitchen island. The kitchen cabinets are standard units, the lowers in maple, the uppers stained blue and green.

OPPOSITE The entry is held up with the trunk of an ash tree painted Chinese red by Jan Mulfinger. The color signals welcome to those who enter. This is the entry used when unpacking and packing the car.

A GOOD MARRIAGE

It's been a "good marriage"—for that is essentially what it is when two couples agree to co-own and share a cabin together as a home away from home.

And it's been a venture and adventure: the day in the middle of winter when we all visited the land at the edge of a large lake with a ravine, large trees, a small, old Finnish log cabin, and an outhouse, and stalking knee-deep through the snow, decided to buy it; the winter weekend a year later in a rented cabin when together we discussed and sketched out a conceptual design for our new abode, which Dale later developed in more detail; the evenings spent in the summer dunking cedar shingles in chocolate brown stain—and in the process staining ourselves—and hanging them up like laundry on clotheslines to dry in our garage and backyard; the week of spring break working together from sunrise to sunset, sanding and polyurethaning the almost-finished cabin from top to bottom twice, until we tumbled exhausted into bed; and, finally, the big day when we trucked up furniture, bedding, china, and kitchen utensils—and moved in and celebrated with our first sumptuous dinner there together.

And it continues to be a journey of wonderful experiences, events, and memories; leaving the city and arriving at the beautiful stillness of nature—water, rocks, trees, and sky; taking a boat ride over the shimmering—or choppy—surface of the lake while eagles soar overhead; having a drink down at the dock watching fishermen, turtles, and waterfowl going about their business while a fiery sunset lights up the golden leaves of fall; enjoying each others' stories and companionship or spending time with respective friends and family; celebrating New Year's around a warm fire among snow-laden pine trees under a cold midnight sky with thousands of stars overhead and deer standing there outside in the moonlight.

It's been one of the best decisions of our life!

—GUNTER AND SUSAN DITTMAR, *the other half of the Mulfinger–Dittmar "marriage"*

We scrapped my idea of an addition and began the design of a totally new structure 50 ft. away. The existing cabin reduced our need for seasonal sleeping spaces but did suggest we might need two bathrooms to handle a crowd. A kitchen, dining and living areas, and a couple of bedrooms were to complete the program, along with a screened porch.

The site we selected has a spectacular view above the treetops but has an elevation difference. We picked a design with the entry level located above the social space, so the kitchen and a bath on the lower level could also serve the log cabin. The design would be banked into the northwest side of the knoll and thus be protected from cold winds while remaining open to the southeast and southwest sun. This passive solar strategy has served us well over these many years.

The forms we used to enclose the space were drawn from vernacular traditions shaped by common framing techniques. Exposure of structural members between levels would add interest to the spaces and give the carpenters an opportunity to showcase their skills. The use of tree trunks for columns would add whimsy to function.

The second-floor Eagle's Nest bedroom has windows at bed level for viewing the distant lake.

We clad the whole interior with local pine, set vertically, with variable board sizes. The pine was also used on the ceilings, except in one bedroom where we stained beaded ceiling boards a vibrant barn red. For the floor, we used inexpensive multicolored slate that picked up the hues of the moss and stone on the site. Kitchen cabinets—clear maple base units and moss green and slate blue upper cabinets—were bought from a big box store. The bathrooms were sheathed in whitewashed pine.

The exterior is clad in cedar shingles stained a deep dark brown and plywood and battens stained light birchbark gray.

We prestained both sides of the panels and shingles to ensure the longevity of the exterior surfaces. Wood windows with metal-clad exteriors in red and teal add a wisp of color and blend in perfectly with the backdrop of nature's hues. The front entry column is painted Chinese red and was my wife's personal statement to welcome all to our happy cabin.

Heating systems at remote building sites need to take advantage of the unique opportunities that can sometimes be found in local utility companies. Our cooperative electrical supplier offered off-peak rates for electrical heating systems employing heat storage. Our system has a series of electric mats set in sand 2 ft. below the slab and two ceramic storage heaters, one on each level. This system is easy to operate and cost-effective, but it has a slow response time. Thus we added a few direct electric baseboard panels at strategic locations for more instantaneous response to take a chill off the house.

A two-sided wood-burning metal-insert fireplace is located in the center of the space to take full advantage of its radiant heat. A local mason created a stone wrap for the firebox using fieldstone we collected from the site. It was then topped with slabs of the recycled fir we also used for the beams.

Our cabin has served us well for more than a decade. We have accommodated over a dozen guests at a time in the summer and half that number in the winter. It is a space of friendship and bonding, easy to maintain, and enjoyable to use. At 1,300 sq. ft., it is all we need for our respite in the forest.

BACK TO THE CABIN

It has been well over a decade since I wrote the first of 72 "Cabin Fever" articles for *Mpls/St.Paul Magazine* and a full decade since publishing *The Cabin* (Taunton Press, 2002). In that time I have had the good fortune at SALA Architects to design over 75 cabins from Nova Scotia to Jackson Hole, Wyoming, for an amazing array of clients. And I have taught more than 150 precocious architecture students the fine art of cabin design. I now come to the subject with new insights and seasoned strategies for the logic, utility, and beauty of cabin design.

My original thinking (reflected in the structures profiled in *The Cabin* and in my own cabin) suggested a 1,200-sq.-ft. limit for all things cabin, although I knew at the time that this might be a bit artificial. I now think the number to be closer to 1,800 sq. ft. before a cabin becomes a lodge, lake home, or getaway retreat. Cabins, to me, still speak of modesty, shared social spaces to encourage the camaraderie of family and friends, and an open, relaxed atmosphere.

There still remains no place in a cabin for a master bedroom suite, a formal entry, an attached garage, or formal dining. Life is simple at a cabin—the mudroom is entry enough for all and burning wood is done for more than just the charm of it.

Most of the principles for designing or remodeling a cabin I laid forth in *Cabinology* (Taunton Press, 2008). But here in *Back to the Cabin* are examples of what I and other designers (and some homeowners) have been doing in cabin design. As before, I searched across North America for new and old ideas worthy of print and found hundreds of great projects. I edited them down to these 37 examples, which demonstrate the breadth of ideas unique to cabins. Some of these themes are tried and true and natural extensions of the traditions of cabin building, while others are fresh, new, and test the boundaries of what it means to cabin. I hope you enjoy the journey.

TO CABIN

Have you ever noticed how the English say, "He's in hospital" or "She's in University"? They drop the article "the." Americans say "the hospital" or "the University." Rather than a noun, "cabin" is a verb, an activity, as in "cabining."

This is the way I think of cabins, although I still use an article, as in "I'm off to the cabin this weekend." It is not the edifice of cabin I retreat to but the activities we do at the cabin.

The entry door is next to the second-floor sleeping loft. The bridge in the foreground accesses the Eagle's Nest bedroom.

The cabins may be old or of new construction making use of tried-and-true ideas. Archetypal cabins remain an iconic

memory in the American psyche, whether it be Abe Lincoln's birthplace, Thoreau's writing studio, or an Adirondack camp. The rich American history of cabins is alive and thriving and remains a dominant force in new cabin creation.

Edwin Lundie positioned his cabins so that the broad side captures the breadth of the big lake view and the end elevation faces the spectacle of the crashing waves on the shore.

"Lundie's projects went together like finely crafted furniture, homes composed in their settings like photographs."

LUNDIE'S LEGACY

With its dramatic rocky shoreline and vast expanse of sky and water, it's not surprising that photographer Olaf Olsen and his wife, Marian, were attracted to the North Shore of Lake Superior. In the late 1940s, the couple purchased a waterfront parcel that jutted into the lake, allowing for panoramic vistas.

For the design of their cabin, the Olsens turned to architect Edwin Lundie, perhaps attracted by the Scandinavian vernacular apparent in the cabins and lodges he had already built in the area. Teamed with craftsman builder Joe Pecore, Lundie designed timber structures modeled after the log and stave folk architecture of rural Norway and Sweden. Although Lundie never saw the inspiration for his designs firsthand, he amassed a substantial reference library, including many scrapbooks documenting specific stylistic attributes. He was noted for his highly detailed drawings, including full-scale templates for carved interior wood details, stone fireplaces, and iron fabrications like hinges, door latches, and light fixtures. Area builders said his projects went together like finely crafted furniture, homes composed in their settings like photographs.

The design Lundie came up with for the Olsens is a four-bent timber frame (see "The Art of Timber Frame Construction" on p. 16), 38 ft. by 28 ft., with a 4-ft. entry balcony extension. All of the living space fronts the water, with two bedrooms and a bath behind. Above the bedrooms and between the timber trusses are two sleeping lofts, accessed from a central staircase. Curtains can be drawn to make them private.

Nine casement windows extend along the lakefront wall of the living room for an expansive view to the southeast. Two more windows on the southwestern wall continue the view down the shore. A stone fireplace occupies the corner between these two walls, allowing the homeowners to gaze upon its flickering flames while enjoying the great lake view beyond. The stone for the fireplace was collected locally and has the same patina as the rock ledges just beyond the cabin.

ABOVE The shore of Lake Superior offers dramatic water views and sunset tranquility. Those who built on it over 60 years ago had access to the greatest sites; the cabin's current owner had a deck plane scribed into the rocks for sitting around the fire pit.

LEFT The cabin sits on a promontory that projects into the lake. Entry is off a cantilevered timberframed balcony on the northeast side of the cabin reminiscent of those found on alpine chalets.

ABOVE The newel posts, stair railing, and dormer detailing exhibit Lundie's signature attention to detail. He directed craftsmen through the use of full-scale template drawings.

RIGHT The dramatic roof structure of the cabin is a four-bent timber frame highlighting the rafters, purlins, queen posts, and cross ties. To the right, the balcony rail protects one of two similar-sized loft sleeping areas. Below, a cozy living room has a corner fireplace with lake views on either side.

The pine cabinets are original to the cabin; the appliances and countertop have been updated.

Lundie included many of his characteristic details in the home: Pine-cone cutouts grace the handrails and there are articulated newel-post heads. A built-in dining hutch is adjacent to the stairs. Iron latches secure "Z" doors and iron butterfly hinges grace cabinet doors.

Board-and-batten siding rings the main floor and horizontal shiplap is used in the gable ends. The gutters and downspouts are constructed of wood and have been recently lined with copper. Three dormers let in light and provide ventilation for the bedroom lofts. The entry balcony is detailed with finely crafted spindles and posts.

Unfortunately, Olaf Olsen had but a few years to enjoy his property before he died, but Marian lived there for several more

The roof load on the rafters is transferred to the purlins, which bear on the queen post, which transfers the load to the cross ties.

THE ART OF TIMBERFRAME CONSTRUCTION

Timber framing is an ancient form of wood construction still in use today. It is commonly characterized by planes of timber trusses resting on posts, the whole assembly referred to as a bent. Individual bents are connected with beams and girts (lateral supports), thus completing the walls of the frame. Above, purlins (horizontal structural members) and ridge beams tie the bents together for the roof. Above the purlins are the rafters, to which the roof sheathing is attached. The frame is made rigid by adding diagonal braces that join the posts, beams, and trusses. The wood timbers are joined together through hidden mortise-and-tenon joints.

Timber frames are beautiful to look at, as anyone will attest who has entered an old timber barn. For this reason, timber structures usually retain some portion of open, high space where the frame can be experienced from the inside.

seasons. Since then, the cabin has had two subsequent owners, both of whom have been mindful stewards of the original Lundie design. George Rumsey, who bought the house from Marian Olsen, built a timbered gate at the highway entrance to the meandering driveway. Current owner Steven Lukas has invested significantly in updating the cabin's electricity and plumbing, in addition to replacing the windows. He has also added landscaping, as well as a garage with a guest suite above.

Today a local historical society offers an annual fundraising tour of the Lundie collection of cabins along the North Shore. The tour ends with a picnic on the shoreline that Olaf and Marian first discovered in the 1940s.

RIGHT The cabin has two bedrooms on the first floor and two sleeping lofts above. The lofts (one of which is shown here) overlook the main living space, from which they can be screened with privacy curtains.

First floor

Bedroom

Bedroom

Balcony

Kitchen

Dining

Living room

Loft

Loft bedroom

Loft bedroom

0   5   10

OPPOSITE The table and benches (designed by Lundie himself) have a prominent corner view.

BELOW The current owner added a garage with a guest studio above, which is designed in the Scandinavian style to blend with Lundie's design for the main cabin.

"It's a little piece of heaven for my fly-fishing husband and the grandkids."

PARKS AND REC REDO

Diana and Dick Beattie spend much of each summer and fall at their D-D homestead in the Beaverhead Range in Montana. At an elevation of 6,400 ft., the property straddles the Continental Divide between Idaho and Montana and borders a national forest. A creek on the property cascades into a series of five ponds, and adjacent to the top pond sits The Soddy, a stone cabin built for day use.

The cabin and ponds are downhill from the mountain house, accessed by a path cut in the wild grasses and lined with an allée of aspens. At The Soddy, young grandchildren learn how to cast off the dock, while parents and friends relax in old Adirondack chairs on the porch. On a hot summer day guests might take a refreshing dip in the cool water of the pond. In the winter they return to The Soddy after cross-country skiing for hot chocolate in front of a crackling fire.

OPPOSITE Diane Beattie wanted her "Soddy" to sit along the bank of a trout pond and look much like the old stone pump house she'd seen in *Park and Recreation Structures*, a 1938 book by Albert Good. The stone path and dock anchor the structure to the setting and the water.

LEFT Fishing in the high Rocky Mountain streams is an artful sport. Taking a break for some reflection and warm coffee adds to the memories, and this porch overlook is the perfect place.

AMERICAN INSPIRATION

Park and Recreation Structures was first published as three volumes in 1938. It was then republished in 1990 by Gray Books as one volume (and is now available from Princeton Architectural Press). It documents in plans and photographs the variety of National Park structures across America, built from local materials (from stone and adobe to logs and milled lumber) using construction methods common to builders of the particular locales. They include bridges, bathhouses, park shelters, cabins, and lodges in a great breadth of styles. This book is an absolute treasure for those seeking design inspiration for their own cabin in the great wild woods.

A warm fireplace takes the chill off the stone walls of The Soddy as well the bones of a fisherman. The stone is from a defunct gold mine nearby.

OPPOSITE TOP Access to the cabin is along a path that passes along the edge of five ponds, all part of a cascading mountain stream.

OPPOSITE BOTTOM The cabin is but a single small room where fishermen can take a break from the cold stream, or a wet day, to relax and tell a tall fish tale. Twig furniture has been selected to stay in tune with the timeless nature of the stone structure.

LEFT A fisherman's creel must have a snack for lunch. The windowsill exhibits the fisherman's competitor, the grizzly bear, as well as the thickness of the stone walls of the cabin.

OPPOSITE/TOP The simplicity of fly-fishing gear adds to the elegance of the sport.

Porch

Living room

0   5   10

Diana Beattie had long been familiar with the book *Park and Recreation Structures* by Albert Good, published in 1938, and was particularly charmed by the Oklahoma Pump House found on page 122. For her soddy she sought not to copy the pump house exactly but rather to create an equally rustic and singular small structure. She engaged architect Candace Tillitson-Miller because of her experience replicating historical styles (including being able to source historically appropriate products and materials) and her ability to tap talented local craftspeople.

The stones used for the project are tailings from a defunct gold-mining operation on the property. Local mason Rod Cranford (now retired) built the structure, which is a single general-use room 12 ft. by 9½ ft. Its walls are two stones' width wide and reinforced vertically and horizontally with rebar for seismic code. There is no running water at The Soddy but it does have electricity, which runs under the floor and through a chase in the stone walls. Atop the 2-ft.-thick walls is a lodge-pole roof structure capped off with sod planted with wildflowers.

"It's a little piece of heaven for my fly-fishing husband and the grandkids," says Diana Beattie of The Soddy. Though the source of its inspiration may have originated in Oklahoma, it feels right at home in Montana.

"On a knoll overlooking a pristine lake stood a little log cabin."

HER DREAM/HIS ENCHANTMENT

Ann Gibbon had been entranced by the idea of life in a log cabin since her youth. But it wasn't until midlife that she and her husband, Guy, decided to act on her dream. One rainy weekend while vacationing in northeastern Minnesota more than 15 years ago, cabin fever set in. The couple decided to see if any log cabins that fit Ann's lifetime of imaginings were for sale. After looking at several log homes with master bedroom suites and attached garages, the first day ended in disappointment.

A day passed and the realtor called with news that an elderly couple was selling an unimproved seasonal log cabin equipped with an outhouse. Ann and Guy rushed to the location down a winding, muddy road. On a knoll overlooking a pristine lake stood a little log cabin. Ann was smitten, but reserved judgment until she could see the interior. "Let's buy it!" she exclaimed to Guy upon stepping inside. Its primitive simplicity seemed channeled right out of her dream. The logs were warm and inviting, the space lifted to the

OPPOSITE An east-facing entry offers a spot to keep kindling dry, while the roof's low overhang is a convenient spot to hang a kerosene lantern. The cabin has electricity, but frequent outages necessitate the use of lanterns and candles.

LEFT A narrow screened porch facing south toward the lake serves as a spot to eat, nap, socialize, or read a book in the fresh air.

A woodstove is central to the cabin space and useful on a chilly morning. The white pine log walls and ceiling rafters are nearly a century old.

Porch

Kitchen

Living room

Bedroom

0   5   10

roof, and the interior was open, an all-inclusive space for cooking, dining, sitting, and sleeping—all this plus a narrow fresh-air screened-in porch from which to watch the loons out on the lake.

Guy was charmed by the cabin as well, but it was an outbuilding standing just 10 ft. from the lapping waves of the lake that particularly delighted him. A 20-ft. by 20-ft. open space, it would be perfect for what Guy had dreamed of, a room of his own for writing, a place he liked to think of as his "Scriptorium." They left to sign papers before anyone else could make an offer.

WHICH WAY DO THE LOGS GO?

There are traditions for both vertically and horizontally positioned logs in cabin construction. The Gibbons' property provides examples of both.

The main cabin is a classic scribed log structure, 18 ft. by 24 ft., made from native white pine trees that were felled on site. The hip roof sits atop 11 courses of logs. Log ties span the short vertical reach of the house, resisting the outward thrust of the roof and providing for loft sleeping space. Low windows were cut in under the top log. A skylight was added to let light stream into the loft and then cascade down into the cabin.

The Scriptorium was built using the stockade-style vertical log wall method (see the photo below). Small logs were attached to the top and bottom boards, called plates. A ridge pole carries the gable rafters across log ties to repel the outward roof thrust. The vertical log method is easier and faster than scribing horizontally positioned logs but historically was usually relegated to sheds and outbuildings. In northern Minnesota, tamarack trees were often employed in this method. It is still used today in cabin building, utilizing plywood splines to secure vertical logs.

A light-filled kitchen favors windows over upper cabinets. The tree trunk above carries the load of the loft.

It turned out that the cabin was built in 1923. The original owner was a forest manager, and a fire tower once stood above the cabin. The other structure, a combination mess hall/bunkroom for summer foresters, was built a few years later. It would take a little elbow grease to clean up the buildings, but Ann and Guy liked them as they were, outhouse and all, and no fancy additions would be necessary.

At the time Ann and Guy bought the cabin, they were both educators, Guy a college professor and Ann a high school teacher, which allowed them three uninterrupted months of enjoyment at the lake. For Ann, this meant country walks, reading books, and meeting new friends.

Guy Gibbon has put a simple writer's table to productive use. The view out to the lake presents the constant temptation of a cool and restorative dip. The clear night sky gives ample opportunity for star-gazing.

The Scriptorium

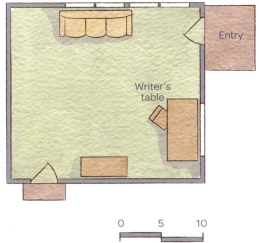

Entry

Writer's table

0   5   10

OPPOSITE The Scriptorium is nicely screened from the shore by pines and shrubs, affording Guy the privacy he needs for his work.

BELOW The log ends highlight their large and small diameters, laid in opposite directions to balance out a near level wall. Window openings are placed away from corners to maintain the structural integrity of the wall.

For Guy, it meant writing books. As a University of Minnesota anthropologist, he had spent many summers on research digs; now he would have time to reflect and write. Two books on Native Americans flowed from the Scriptorium. Now retired (as is Ann), Guy has just completed *The Archaeology of Minnesota: A Guide to the Prehistory of the Upper Mississippi River Region*, and he knows there are more books to follow. Each summer morning Guy leaves for work 30 paces away from Ann's dream cabin. In the evening he returns to sit with her on the screened porch to reflect on the day's accomplishments.

At twilight, the guest cabin barn glows like a beacon, and the expanses of glass make it look as though the siding has been peeled away.

"The hayloft has been converted to a bedroom that looks out onto the glass wall."

BARN LIFE

John Marsh always wanted a barn. He grew up in New England playing in barns with his cousins. His family was in the building trade and it was while he was apprenticing as a carpenter that he began to truly appreciate the elegance of early New England barns. Although college led to a different profession, in finance, Marsh retained "an interest in architecture and a keen eye for simple traditional structures."

Years later, after John and his wife, Anne Winton, had relocated to Sun Valley, Idaho, his dream of a barn of his own was revived when he met Ken Epworth, owner of The Barn People, a Vermont-based barn-recycling company. Epworth was working on a project nearby when they struck up a conversation about the prospects of finding a small barn that could be relocated to the property next to the Marsh residence. A few months later, Epworth, now back in Vermont, called to say that he had found just the right barn.

John had followed the work of local architect Candace Tillotson Miller, appreciating "her scale, proportion, and use of traditional materials" in homes and guest cabins in the Rocky Mountain region. Her work featured recycled material, sometimes repurposing entire buildings. With Miller and Epworth, John thought he had the perfect team for creating a guest-cabin barn he could gaze out upon from the window of his home office.

LEFT The cabin is oriented to capture a view across the meadow to the Pioneer Mountain Range beyond. Appropriately enough, the framing members frame the view.

BELOW The barn doors retain the rustic character appropriate to a utilitarian building.

A small kitchenette is adequate enough to prepare breakfast or a snack. The barn theme extends to the wood used for the cabinet doors, while the ceiling is the exposed structure of the loft.

First floor

Loft

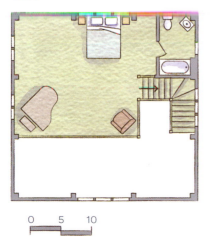

0   5   10

After being dismantled, shipped across country to its new home, and reassembled, the 200-year-old barn got a new "skin" built out a few inches all the way around it. Barn siding was never intended for use in heated structures, so when a barn is repurposed to be a domicile it needs a new warm skin to which new outer siding can be attached; for timber frames these skins are usually constructed from SIPS—a sandwich of rigid insulation with plywood—or OSB, oriented stand board. This skin also weatherizes and insulates the home, and square cuts can be made into it to install energy-efficient windows. As John wryly notes, the old timber frame and siding end up functioning as "expensive wallpaper." But he loves the timeless timbers, particularly the diagonal bracing. The new exterior accommodates an eastern wall, made predominantly of glass where the diagonal braces are backlit by the glass beyond it, with a view to the Pioneer Mountain Range, with 15 peaks over 11,500 ft. tall.

The original barn, a 30-ft. by 30-ft. structure, had three 10-ft. bays with a hayloft above. One bay was removed to use as a garage and storage area. One bay is opened at the eastern end of the space so John can look up to see the full height of the frame rising

LEFT A radiant-heated floor provides a toasty level of comfort even with the large expanses of glass.

OPPOSITE TOP The diagonal braces on the Z-doors keep the vertical boards of the door from racking.

OPPOSITE BOTTOM The loft bedroom is sufficiently large to house a piano where Anne Winton can practice.

BARN PEDIGREE

The Vermont Barn People reassembled the barn, compete with its mortise, and, tenon joints.

John's barn was originally built by the Kidder family in 1820 in the village of Bradford, Vermont. It is a small version of a classic Yankee three-bay barn, a design that came over from England. This type of barn was originally designed for grain storage (the word "barn" derives from Old English and meant "barley house" or "barley enclosure"). Its use for housing animals evolved over time, and the Kidder barn was last used to keep horses.

The barn was built by a master framer from old-growth hemlock felled on the Kidder property. The workmen shaped and hewed the timbers with broadaxes and adzes, adding mortises and tenons with mallets and chisels. Holes were drilled into the timbers using an auger and made to receive interlocking hardwood pegs of maple and oak.

The frame was assembled into "bents" on the ground, and each bent was hefted into place using long poles and many helpers. Such a barn raising was a community event (and still is in Amish and Mennonite communities around the country) heralded with revelry and a home-cooked feast.

27 ft. in the air. The hayloft has been converted to a bedroom that looks out onto the glass wall. By limiting almost all of the windows to the large eastern opening, the exterior of the barn retains its barn character, clad in weathered wood.

The project was completed over a decade ago and Anne and John have found the barn to be a perfect getaway for visiting family and friends. Anne has taught modern dance classes in its main space and she contemplates adding a pottery studio some day. It is also, of course, a great space to escape to with a good book on a rainy day.

"Camps are old clothes, fishing poles, wooden boats, creaky buildings, moss on the roof, and critters under the porch."

ADIRONDACK CAMP

The Adirondacks in upstate New York have a rich architectural history of cabins, lodges, and other retreat buildings. Architect Nils Luderowski specializes in updating retreats with modern-day conveniences. From his firsthand knowledge of the Great Camps (see "Adirondack Architecture" on p. 42) and other lesser-known retreats, he translates the scale, details, and materials of this legacy style.

The objective for this project was to create a cozy camp for two, but one that possessed some of the defining characteristics of the Adirondack camp style. Luderowski's grasp of the Shingle style and his use of local stone and wood, as well as rich, deep color, fit the dreams his clients had for their cabin.

The couple had been visiting the property they intended to build on for 15 years and were well aware of the site's specific limitations but significant opportunities. Code required them to build within the footprint of a seasonal structure that was being replaced. This size limit would help contain their budget.

OPPOSITE Coffee on the porch with a lake view is a great way to start the morning. The wall is detailed to express mass, while the arches soften the rectilinear lines. The thickness of the corner walls provides the opportunity for built-in shelves.

LEFT The living room and a small porch look out over the lake. The second-floor roof has a gentle roll characteristic of historic Adirondack structures.

LEFT Food prep becomes easy in this light-filled and efficiently laid out kitchen. A trellis cloud disguises the lighting at the ceiling.

OPPOSITE The corner fireplace straddles the forest and lake views.

First floor

Entry

Kitchen

Bedroom

Porch

Living room

0   5   10

Luderowski developed a plan with the main living space and primary bedroom on the main level, with all the rooms facing the water. The living space was positioned facing south to capture the trickle of tree-filtered summer light, which turned into a flood of sunshine during the warmth-starved winter months.

To get the most out of a small plan, Luderowski designed a center-hall entry and stair. The open stairway makes the living room seem bigger than it really is. The second floor steps in a few feet from the main floor below. High interior windows into the stairwell borrow light from the bedrooms, which then cascades down into the darker interior of the cabin. The cabin has the solid corners and centered windows characteristic of Shingle-style Adirondack buildings. The wood shingles are stained dark green, allowing the cabin to blend into the forest.

ADIRONDACK ARCHITECTURE

No single area in America is as well known for its rustic vernacular architecture as the Adirondacks in upstate New York. In the bucolic setting of mountains, forests, and pristine lakes, the wealthy created a plethora of enclaves of retreat buildings meant predominantly for summer and fall use that came to be known as the Great Camps. Developed in the late 1800s, Adirondack architecture has been widely copied across North America in the form of cabins, cottages, and lodges ever since.

Adirondack-style buildings are rarely ostentatious, but rather employ a wilderness ethic and conservative aesthetic. "Camps are old clothes, fishing poles, wooden boats, creaky buildings, moss on the roof, and critters under the porch," cites Paul Malo in his foreword to the book *Adirondack Camps*. Local materials—logs, branches, birch bark, and stone—were used in the construction of many of the original buildings. Others utilized milled lumber and shingles to add a modicum of refinement.

Camp structures were embellished by local craftsmen with forged metal brackets, latches, and light fixtures. Lampshades were produced from deer hides and chandeliers from antlers. Prize catches and game trophies, along with well-worn oars and snow shoes, adorned the walls. "There are varying degrees of rusticity possible," notes Ann Stillman O'Leary in *Adirondack Style*. "One could use silk velvet ocelot print or a cotton buffalo plaid to upholster the same piece."

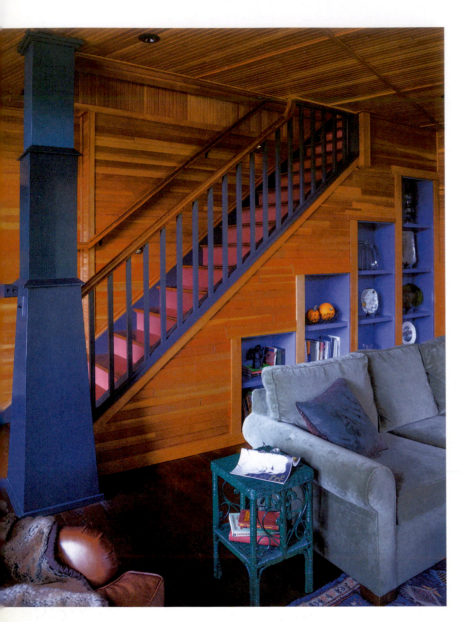

Storage is conveniently captured under the stair. The interior is a harmonious blend of fir and colorfully painted wood. The structural column that supports the center of the cabin presents an additional opportunity to add color.

LEFT With the tub wrapped in windows opening to the surrounding forest, taking a bath is almost an alfresco experience.

BELOW Lakeside cabins have back doors usually convenient for entering from the driveway and garage. This one is charmed by details that echo the lake façade.

Second floor

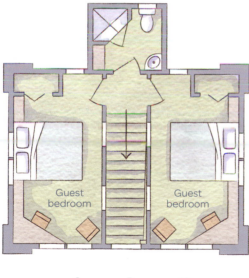

Guest bedroom

Guest bedroom

0   5   10

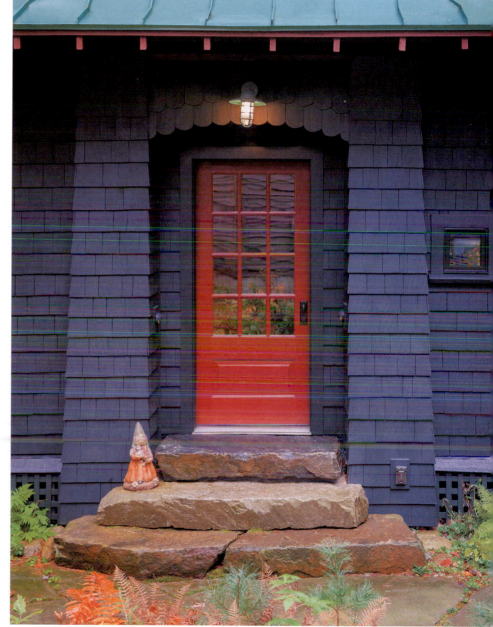

> "Atop the tower is a covered observation deck, perfect for enjoying long views out over the fields."

BIRD'S EYE

Northern California has a rich architectural history of water towers, both in the hilly wine country and the flat farmland. Irrigation is central to the success of California crops, and before today's high-pressure systems it was provided by the 30-ft. towers that still dot the landscape.

Living in the Bay Area, the Butler family wanted to purchase farmland where they could reconnect with their agrarian roots (Mrs. Butler had grown up on a farm in Southern California) and try their hand at growing their own fruits, vegetables, and grains. Over a period of years, they purchased three parcels in Yolo County, west of Sacramento. Here they began to raise tomatoes, corn, sunflowers, and other crops, along with a herd of sheep. Soon they felt the need to replace the trailer home they had been using as temporary housing with a permanent structure. Their son, Lewis, an architect in San Francisco, was commissioned to design a cabin where they could conduct business but that could also serve as a weekend escape for extended family.

OPPOSITE The tower houses a bedroom area and is crowned with a covered observation deck.

LEFT The Butler family sought a cabin for relaxation at their country farm. An observation deck atop the tower affords a panoramic view over their fields.

ABOVE The cabin is a marriage of two iconic forms: the shed and the tower, this one inspired by historic local water towers.

OPPOSITE The living room has a woodstove for warming up chilly mornings. To the rear, a sleeping loft is perched above a bathroom and closet.

First floor

Loft

Living room

Porch

Bedroom

Deck

0   5   10

The Butlers concluded there was no ideal site for the cabin on the property they currently owned, but rather than wait for an appropriate parcel to become available they asked Lewis to design the structure so it could be moved.

Before Lewis could put pen to paper, his father came to him with photos of 20 historic water towers from the region and proclaimed, "I want something like these." When Lewis showed his father sketches of a few designs that used the towers for inspiration, he retorted, "No, I want something historically correct, as if it had always been there."

Lewis began again, this time with a classic tapered-wall tower with a lean-to chicken coop shed form nestled next to it. The shed houses the communal living space, the kitchen, a sleeping loft above a bathroom, and a closet, as well as a covered porch with a view to the south. In the base of the tower is the principal bedroom, with 15-ft.-high ceiling walls that gradually slant inward. Atop the tower is a covered observation deck, perfect for enjoying long views out over the fields.

The exterior surfaces are intended to fit in with the vernacular buildings of the area. The shed is sheathed in the stained, square-edged vertical siding common to local barns. The tower has tapered lap siding painted white, similar to water towers in the region. Both structures are roofed in corrugated metal.

The interior walls and ceilings are paneled with vertical-grain fir plywood, with matching built-in cabinets. The floor is finished in 1-ft. by 3-ft. cork tiles. A dark green enameled woodstove provides all the heat necessary for winter use.

The cabin sits surrounded by cultivated fields, where the smell of newly tilled earth meets the odor of diesel fuel. From the observatory tower, the Butlers can look upon the literal fruits of their labor: heavy-laden tomato plants, stands of wheat swaying in the breeze, and bright sunflowers with their heads turned toward the sun.

ABOVE A spiral stair floats inside an open shaft and gives access to the rooftop overlook.

LEFT The cabin has a full kitchen with ample built-in storage. The fir plywood used for the cabinets matches the wood of the walls and ceiling, giving a sense of unity to the interior. Northern light from the clerestory windows above floods the room.

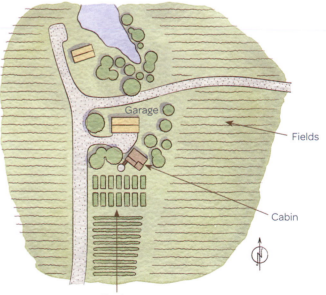

Garage

Fields

Cabin

Garden

TALL DREAMS

A tower is an intriguing feature to consider for a cabin, but the form presents some challenges. First, its interior taper is at odds with a homeowner's desire for living space. Also, the need for a code stairway inside the tower often enlarges it beyond desired proportions. The Butler tower achieves its gracefulness in part by locating the stairs outside the form. Although the tower appears to taper in all directions, two sides do not, which facilitates the juncture of the shed and tower.

Zoning codes often restrict residential structures to a height of 30 ft. or 35 ft. from the ground to the top of the roof. A four-story tower can be attained in 32 ft., leaving a foot to the ground and 2 ft. for a sloping roof.

ABOVE Any closeness one might feel with the tapering of the walls in the tower bedroom is offset by its high ceiling.

TOP RIGHT The lean-to shed form contains the living room and kitchen, as well as a porch. It is built on piers and supported by two large glulam beams, which will allow it to be moved in the future, if desired.

RIGHT The porch looks out over the family vegetable garden, where produce can be picked fresh for dinner.

The barn was remodeled to include living space in the upper-level haymow. A ramp was built for access by all.

> "Our guests traipse up the ramp, open the door, and bingo, you see it."

BACKYARD HIDEAWAY

We usually imagine cabins being set in remote locations, such as a forest, alongside a lake, or atop a mountain. But they can also reside in a backyard in the city. And that is just where you will find Gene Frey's personal retreat, within sight of his kitchen window.

When Gene and Mary Frey became empty nesters, they built a new home in a suburb of Minneapolis. Adjacent to their property was an overgrown wood lot with a small red barn hidden away on it. Gene would look out his window and see the barn and dream of a little hideaway, one where he could watch football with the boys, maybe even smoke a cigar.

Several years in a row Gene approached the owner to see if she would sell, but to no avail. It turned out that she had been fearful that Gene's real intention was to clear-cut the property and build another house. But eventually his persistence paid off; after agreeing that he would preserve the barn for at least seven years, the lot was his.

I had worked with Gene and his family on other architectural ventures and he sought my help on this project. He wanted a

ABOVE Gene coveted the barn he saw on his neighbor's property from his window each day. Eventually he bought it.

LEFT This modest kitchenette was built to share a common plumbing wall with the bathroom behind it.

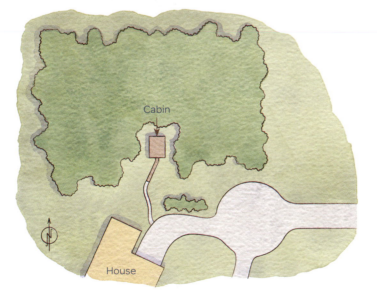

bathroom and game room built into the haymow; the lower level would be dedicated to gardening and lawn equipment storage. The structure would require lots of TLC, as well as the addition of insulation, new electrical, and hook-ups to municipal water, sewer, and gas systems. With an adult son in a wheelchair, the getaway would also need a ramp.

We came up with a design that achieved all of that, but still I thought it needed something special, the WOW factor. Opposite the entry, we replaced the north wall with an all-glass curtain wall that looks out into the surrounding trees. As Gene notes, "Our guests traipse up the ramp, open the door, and bingo, you see it."

OPEN TO ALL

Cabins can easily be made accessible to wheelchair-bound users with a little planning and forethought. Eliminating stairs to an entry door is the place to start. Also important to consider is door width. Front doors are usually at least 36 in. wide, which allows for easy wheelchair access, as opposed to side and interior doors, which can be 32 in. wide and make for very tight maneuvering.

For a wheelchair-accessible bathroom, plan for 48 in. of turning room, as well as grab bars for aid in dismounting the chair. If an existing bathroom can't accommodate 48 in., another option is to have the bathroom door swing out from the room.

For the kitchen, a built-in table should be tall enough so a wheelchair can pull under it.

Finally, for a two-story structure, consider adding an elevator to your plan instead of ramps, which require more real estate and can end up being more costly. An elevator requires only 5 sq. ft.

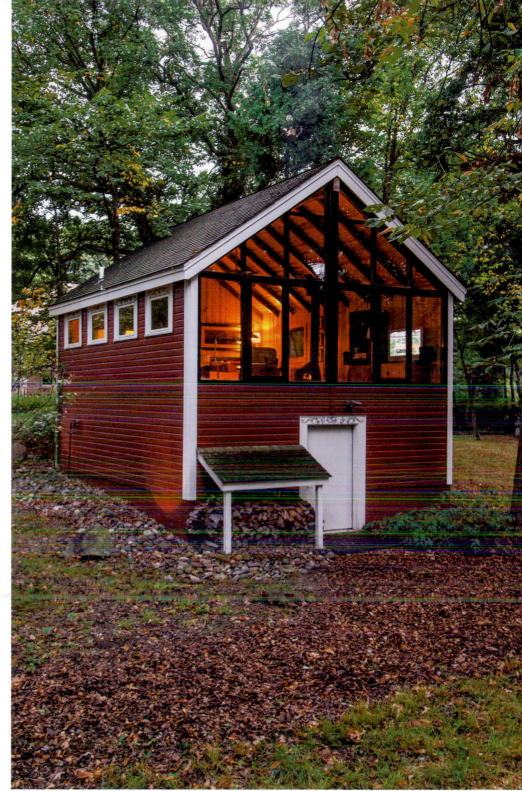

RIGHT An industrial glass curtain wall has replaced the gable end of the barn.

Builder Mike Knutson started work on the remodeling only to find that the barn was essentially a rotted shell sitting on a cracked foundation. So, with Gene's OK, he tore it down. But before the previous owner could complain, an exact replica took its place, perhaps just a few inches higher and a foot or so wider. The red paint with white trim was matched to the old boards, and even the decorative Scandinavian rosemaling painting was replicated on the door and window frames.

With the new view into the woods, Gene soon realized he needed to eradicate the insidious buckthorn as well as add a few pine trees and a path into the forest. He encourages his neighbors to take strolls through his preserve, which is home to a large collection of bird life, including a hoot owl.

The horses along with the hay are long gone from Gene's bucolic barn, where baseball games are viewed and riotous poker games ensue. Seven years have come and gone and there is no talk of barn removal.

OPPOSITE The glass wall that opens out to the surrounding woods makes the 16-ft. by 22-ft. living space appear even larger.

ABOVE Family and friends can enjoy a raucous poker game beside a crackling fire.

Many existing cabins need to be brought into the 21st century with modern conveniences and/or the addition of more space. **ADD AND UPGRADE** Whether extending the seasons of a cabin or better serving the family, such changes need not co-opt charm. This may be a minor modification or a full-fledged transformation, but planning is key for great, long-lasting results.

The old entry was retained in the renovation of the cabin. It was part of the shed roof addition built onto the cabin shortly after it was constructed in 1937.

"The piano has a new home in the living room with plenty of space for family and friends to gather around in harmony."

SING ALONG

Mary and Jim Krook were charmed by the old log cabin the moment they purchased it in 1983. It is located on a clear, spring-fed lake in northwestern Wisconsin that is part of a water system that eventually finds its way to the Gulf of Mexico. They bought the property from the Scalise family, who had enjoyed the home for nearly 50 years.

The old cabin quickly became a summer oasis for the Krooks and their three children, as well as extended family and friends. Over time it came to be kitted out with 10 beds to accommodate the steady flow of visitors. There wasn't much privacy but there was a lot of fun. A piano that sat out on the porch allowed for sing-alongs and, as the children grew, the cabin became a favorite destination for prom night sleepovers, prenuptial parties, and Fourth of July revelry.

Twenty years ago, the Krooks decided to build a home for themselves and move to the property full time. The cabin became the auxiliary bunkhouse for adult children, their spouses, friends, and eventually grandchildren. However, not everyone was charmed by the old cabin's rusticated character, especially after a family of

325 Sauk Trail
Park Forest, Illinois 60466

October 3, 1990

Dr. James (and Mary) Krook MD
c/o Duluth Medical Clinic
Duluth, Missesota

Dear Dr. Krook:

I think that this letter and its contents will come as a surprise
to you and to your wife, whom I know were the purchasers of a little
more than 35 acres of wooded land on Bony Lake, Town of Barnes,
from a now deceased Chicago attorney, Peter R; Scalise. My wife
suggested, and I quickly agreed, that it would be nice if I could
visit, after many years of being away, the log cabin that my two
brothers, Robert F. and Kenneth D., built on Bony Lake during the
summers between classes at New Trier High School in Winnetka, Ill-
inoise and my oldest brother Bob, at the University of Missouri.
We drove in a model T Ford, which we had put in good running condition, pulling a two wheeled trailer we had built, from Winnetka,
Illinois, to Hayward, and then on to Bony Lake to build a 20' X 20'
main cabin structure plus a kitchen 'L'. The logs had been cut
and "naked"in to us, 20' x 8" X 12" butt diameter, through the efforts
of Tom McClaine, another legendary woodsman, and we commenced construction the first summer, I think in 1937. We dug the holes for
the concrete piers and fireplace base and which we had hand mixed,
cutting and shaping the logs, installation of windows and doors,
roof and floor, driving our own drinking water pipe well, We slept
the first summer or two under a tentin the cleared construction area,
cooked on an old cast iron cook stove, tried to fend off the man-
eating mosquiroes with largely ineffective repellents. Our old
scow of a wood row boat, dubbed Tinton Tessie, afforded us our only
opportunity to fish in the open water altho we were too busy to do
much of that - the big Walley was never caught. I still have the tac-
le box and lures that I used, the rod and Shakespeare reel is now
the property of our grandson in Michigan.

Much of the time during the summers we had the help and company of
one sixteen of the other of two good, school, neighborhood, friends,
although no other professional, carpentry or building help was used.
The storied Tom McClaine used to stop in occasionally to see how
we were getting along and through his good efforts we were guided
to reliable suppliers and sources for hardware, windows and cement
and etc. The chimney and fireplace was built by the highly re-
spected stone mason, Hank Kahler, a few summers after we have completed the original structure, and by that time all of were in the
military service in WW II from 1942 to the end of the war.

While visiting the cabin during the week of 8X 9/11 - 9/13 last,
I stole one of the large granite stones which Hank Kahler didn't use
in the chimney/fireplace or skirting around/under the bottom sill
logs. It is a roundish, reddish/gray stone which weighs 45 lbs.

ABOVE This letter left a few years ago by one of the builders
of the original cabin convinced the Krooks to renovate and
preserve the building, not raze it and start anew.

LEFT Even a small cabin can have room for a piano. Now at
home in the living room, it used to reside on the sleeping porch.

OPPOSITE Now fully enclosed to
create interior living space, the
original lakeside sleeping porch was
constructed with vertical logs, a
method commonly used by French
fur trappers.

It was the lake that attracted the Krooks to this location, first to spend their summers, and then to move to the property full time.

mice was discovered there. The Krooks knew the time had come to rethink their guest quarters. The question was, should they tear it down and build it new or renovate the cabin, restoring and refurbishing it? A serendipitous letter left at their door resolved the conflict.

The letter was from Edward Greenhalgh, who had returned, while the Krooks were away, to see what he and his brothers, Robert and Kenneth, had constructed in the summer of 1937. On summer break from high school and college, they had traveled from Illinois in a Model T with a tent, tools, and some basic provisions. By the end of the summer a 20-ft. by 20-ft. log cabin with a kitchen lean-to had been completed for the Scalise family. With this knowledge in hand, the Krooks knew that restoration and rejuvenation were in order.

OPPOSITE The single room that comprised the original 1937 log cabin is now the living room. As part of the renovation, the interior logs were cleaned and lightened. The original fireplace was fitted with an energy-efficient insert firebox.

RIGHT The dining space is now located in what was the old sleeping porch, with a view to the lake.

BELOW As part of the redesign of the house, a narrow bunkroom was created out of some of the space from the old porch.

The original structure had been added to over the years. First came two bedrooms to the west, followed by an 8-ft. sleeping porch that extended the length of the lake side of the cabin. Eventually a bathroom replaced one of the bedrooms and a laundry room was tucked into the northwest corner.

As part of the renovation, the Krooks have converted the sleeping porch into interior space. Part of it is now the dining area, the remainder a bunkroom and children's play area. Because the main house is equipped with a laundry, the northwest corner of the old house was converted into a modern kitchen. The old kitchen now serves as the entryway to the cabin, with plenty of storage space for snowshoes and ski boots.

Kitchen

Entry

Bedroom

Living room

Children's area

Dining

0 5 10

Original cabin

Addition 3

Kitchen

Addition 1

Living/dining/ sleeping

Addition 2

ABOVE What used to be a dark utility room is now a cheery, light-filled kitchen with a view back to the main house.

OPPOSITE With the cabin now used in all seasons, space was created at the entry for coat and boot storage, as well as a convenient built-in seat for taking shoes off.

The Krooks wanted to be able to use the cabin year-round: Insulation, energy-efficient windows, and a new furnace have made that possible. The old fireplace, with its tendency to smoke, was fitted with a high-performance wood-burning insert. New electrical service was installed, along with better lighting. The floor was leveled and new ash hardwood installed. The logs and ceiling were stripped of their dark varnish and years of soot, and new furniture completed the renovation. And the piano? It has a new home in the living room with plenty of space for family and friends to gather around in harmony.

"Some maintain that it was the cabin of a chauffeur, at the call of nearby wealthy summer residents."

ADDING CHARM

Sometimes the only addition an older cabin needs is a little bit of charm. That is just the project David and Kay Root commenced when they purchased a historic log cabin a few miles from their primary residence. Kay had loved the structure since childhood, and in 1995 she noticed a "for sale" sign in the yard. To her dismay, the interior was not in keeping with what she had imagined it to be, but, undaunted, she was convinced that, with a vision, energy, and the help of several subcontractors, her dream cabin was achievable.

The date of the cabin's construction and its original purpose remain open to local speculation. Its location on the lot, low and off to the side, suggests it might have been a secondary building, the main house perhaps having been demolished or never even been built. Some maintain that it was the cabin of a chauffeur, at the call of nearby wealthy summer residents. But to Kay the facts were less important than returning the interior of the cabin to a time reflecting a slower pace of life.

OPPOSITE Owner Kay Root has loved this historic log cabin since her youth and was lucky enough to be able to purchase the property as an adult.

67

The original claw-foot tub was restored and is a favorite of guests.

With that goal, the cleanup crew commenced stripping away the tacky carpet and worn sheet vinyl. The flooring, which had rotted, was replaced with knotty pine to replicate the original. A 1970s' kitchen peninsula was scaled back to make room for a modest dining table. The kitchen cabinets were refreshed with a new coat of paint and a pot rack was added for cooking convenience.

The systems desperately needed upgrading. The Roots sought to extend the seasonal use of the house by adding insulation and energy-efficient windows. A new furnace and central air-conditioning increased comfort. Electrical wiring was upgraded and decorative lights added in the living and dining areas. The plumbing was improved and a small sink installed in the tiny bathroom. The original claw-foot bathtub was a gem worth retaining and completely in keeping with Kay's dream of lazy days at the cabin.

ONE CABIN'S EVOLUTION

Cabin plans evolve and change over time as new owners adapt structures to fit their changing lifestyles and needs. The Roots believe the oldest section of their getaway is an 18-ft. by 28-ft. portion of the cabin and that it was origi-nally one large space. A potbellied stove is thought to have sat in the middle of the room. As the cabin was subdivided into bedrooms and kitchen, a fireplace with heating baffles was added. It sits askew to take advantage of the flue of an earlier wood-burning kitchen stove and to aim the flames into the living room. An outhouse was replaced with a bath-room and a later addition expanded the kitchen around the plumbing stack.

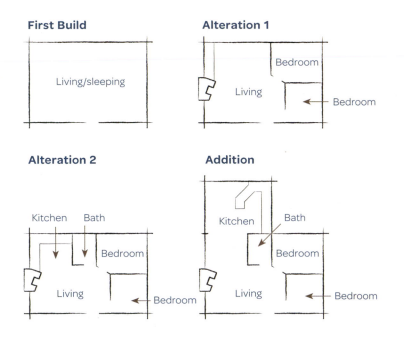

First Build

Living/sleeping

Alteration 1

Bedroom

Living

Bedroom

Alteration 2

Kitchen   Bath

Bedroom

Living

Bedroom

Addition

Kitchen

Bath

Bedroom

Living

Bedroom

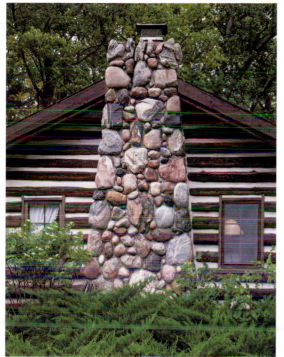

ABOVE Owner Kay Root collected rocks from near and far to be included in the restoration of the chimney.

RIGHT Skylights were added to let light into what had been a dark living space.

ABOVE Writing on the wall is encouraged here, creating a one-of-a-kind built-in guest book.

LEFT The kitchen counters float out into the room so that the existing windows in the log wall need not be disturbed.

Dining

Kitchen

Bath

Bedroom

Living

Bedroom

0   5   10

The outside of the cabin saw little change other than new stone bases to the porch columns, new skylights, and some landscaping. The cedar logs have been recently restained to freshen up the getaway.

The cabin is now an oasis where Kay can drop in for a cup of coffee and a quiet place to read a book. It's also a place of longer stays for friends and family on vacation for a few weeks in Michigan's playground or passing through for a weekend wedding. Now when Kay drives by the cabin, she knows her dream is realized, inside and out.

ABOVE Alternating logs of smaller and larger diameter are critical to the stability of the walls of a log house. This effect is best seen at the corners. Here the logs are shown from the interior, as well as outside the cabin. The dark log color comes from the use of creosote as an early wood preservative.

RIGHT New chinking between the logs presents contrasting stripes as a decorative note to the wall of the back porch.

> "I love the outdoor shower, the expanded view, the wildlife out our front door."

ACCESS TO WATER

The lakeside community of Elkins, New Hampshire, has been the vacation destination of a Boston couple for two decades. First as renters, then buying a home in the village, Sheri and Gerry enjoy the town's relaxed way of life: water activities in the summer, hiking in the autumn colors, and skiing in winter. In addition, there is the local farmer's market, a theater, restaurants, and a spirited ambiance created by the proximity of several colleges. All in all, it is a delightful escape just 90 miles away from their primary residence.

Although their house in Elkins was on a pond, they longed for a lakeside experience. When a small cottage with a beach became available just a quarter mile away, they snatched it up.

The property had originally been one of a group of 11 seasonal rental cottages known as the Rocky Point Cottages; when the owner died, the family subdivided the property. Its prior owner was an Elkins legend of sorts; she had been postmistress for a

OPPOSITE The beach cottage provides storage for water toys below, a living space on the main floor, and loft sleeping above in a charming structure nestled in the trees.

LEFT The owners wanted easy access to Pleasant Lake and got it when they scored a beachfront cabin with a balcony view of the lake. Now the opportunities for kayaking, clambakes, and a refreshing swim are just outside their front door.

The living room is a great place to relax after a strenuous kayak workout and a refreshing swim. The refurbished space blends a newly sanded pine floor, painted walls, and the original rustic wood ceiling.

Modest storage and a place to sit just inside the entry are welcome amenities in any cabin.

time and was known for giving every new resident of the village a copy of *Reflections in the Millpond* by Larry Wood, who, in its pages, coined the phrase, "Home is where the heart is." With such history, Sheri and Gerry decided to restore and remodel the cottage, while simultaneously planning for a future larger home for themselves on the site.

They hired architect Jeremy Bonin of nearby New London, New Hampshire, to make sure the property was adequate for their future plans and also to assist in the cottage renovation. Sheri notes, "We asked him to make the space as open as possible to the views while reusing as much of the existing structure as possible. Being on the water, we had to pull a considerable number of permits and Bonin helped a great deal in navigating the process."

Bonin's scheme for the cottage was to remove many of the interior partition walls and ceilings, creating a cathedral ceiling under the roof for a more open feel. He reused and repositioned windows and doors for better views and ventilation. He salvaged and refinished framing lumber, tongue-and-groove paneling, and wood flooring. New materials were selected for their sustainability; even the woodstove is recycled.

Bonin's efforts won his firm two American Institute of Architecture, New Hampshire, Excellence in Design Awards in 2011, a Merit Award and the People's Choice Award. The jury noted that the project was an "understated, simple, cost-effective renovation making excellent use of space. It speaks to the desire for simplicity in all of us."

Outdoor shower

Entry

Kitchen

Living room

Screened porch

0   5   10

The unfinished loft above the living room provides ample (albeit Spartan) space for overnight guests...and a view over the living room below.

PRESERVING A SENSE OF PLACE

The village of Elkins, New Hampshire, has a rich, historical background. It was originally a mill town called Scytheville and later a summer camp retreat. The Rocky Point Cottages were an integral part of this legacy.

During the remodeling and restoration of the cottage, great care was taken not to disturb the ecosystem and pristine quality of Pleasant Lake and its shoreline. Minimal change to the exterior of the cottage preserves its profile in the landscape, and renovation of its interior gives the cottage a new chapter in New Hampshire history.

Says Sheri, "Our life at the lake is quiet and enjoyable. We hang out at the beach, and take the kayaks, canoe, or wooden motor boat out." Her girls enjoy camping on the beach and Sheri likes "staying down at the cottage for dinner and, at sunset, taking an evening cruise. The cottage gives us so many more reasons to head up to the lake for the weekend. I love the outdoor shower, the expanded view, the wildlife out our front door, and even a warm woodstove in the middle of winter after skating in the cove."

ABOVE An outdoor shower helps to keep sand out of the house.

RIGHT A tranquil view of the lake can be experienced at dusk.

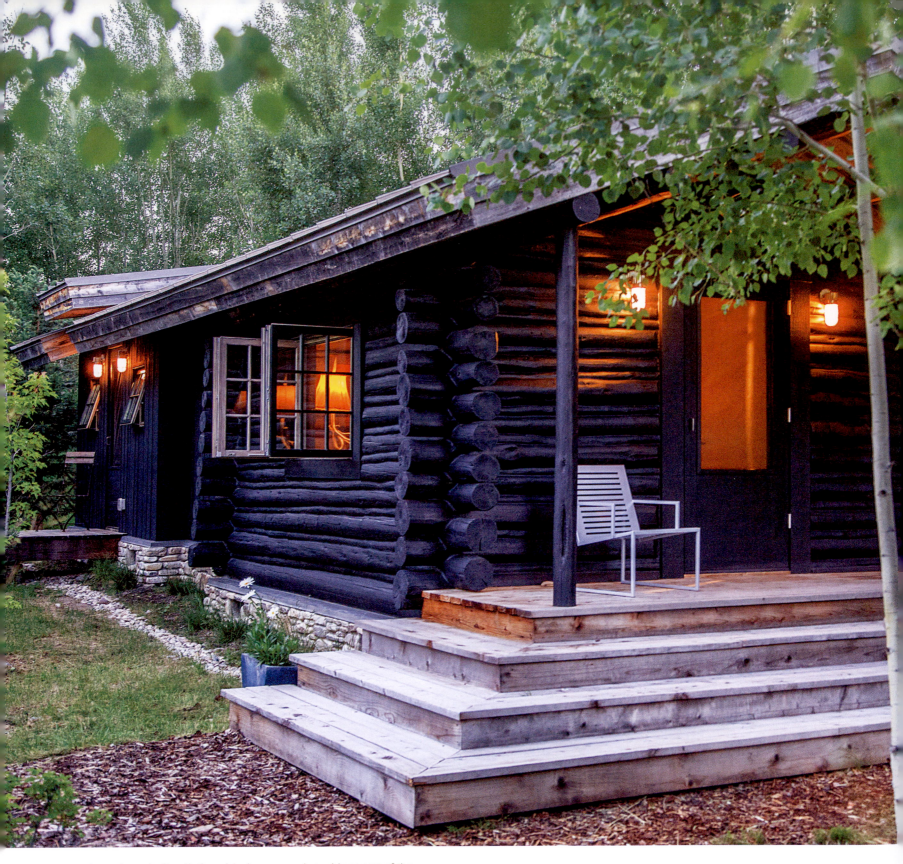

A porch was built onto the original one-room log cabin as part of the renovation. You can see where the addition begins to the back left of the structure.

"I sought to preserve a piece of Jackson Hole history."

SIMPLE ELEGANCE

Larry and Linda Perlman purchased their log home outside of Jackson, Wyoming, to enjoy the outdoor pleasures of hiking, fly fishing, skiing, and gazing at the spectacular Teton mountains. The site was barren of trees, so they embarked on a reforestation plan that would frame vistas to Fish Creek below and the mountains beyond. The plan also included identifying a site for a future guest cabin, which they considered a distant dream.

The auction of old cabins from the historic (and local) Crescent H Dude Ranch gave Linda just the inspiration she was looking for. "I sought to preserve a piece of Jackson Hole history," she said. She purchased one of the 1920s-era log structures and had it relocated to their property, where it has a prime view of the Tetons. Linda asked architect Andy Ankeny to add a bedroom and bath to the small one-room cabin. They had worked together previously and Andy appreciated that Linda "breathed life into projects." Together they envisioned new and old bonded together with a unifying stone base and a single color, inside and out: classic black.

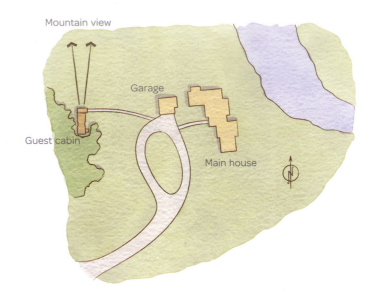

ABOVE The conventionally framed addition (at left) is slipped inside the overlapping log tails of the original cabin. All are painted black for unity.

BELOW The sitting room is in the old log cabin where the logs have been pickled gray. The sliding barn door that leads to the bedroom is surfaced in bonderized steel (the same material used on the roof).

Mountain view

Garage

Guest cabin

Main house

The cabin site was selected for its view of the Teton Range...not a bad choice.

The cabin is a contrast in rusticity and elegance, and no more so than in the modest bath. Here, a Carrara marble vanity and shower coexist with repurposed barn wood and stones that Linda culled from the nearby stream to use as drawer pulls.

The new roof is bonderized steel, and was installed using standing seams. In this case, bonderized metal was chosen not in preparation for painting the roof but for the powdery rusted patina it will develop, a common characteristic of western ranch roofs.

Although the cabin's principal inhabitants are guests, Larry and Linda sneak over when in search of a quiet place to read. But most of the time they make their way over to its small porch at the end of the day so they can watch the sun set on Grand Teton and listen to the gurgle of Fish Creek in the distance, all to the applause of the whispering aspen leaves all around them.

The bedroom includes a built-in window seat and bookshelves, a perfect place to snuggle up and read. The walls are clad in old barn siding.

New

Kitchen

Bedroom

Living room

Deck

0   5   10

The flooring in the living room is wide-plank Douglas fir painted black. The window trim was pickled.

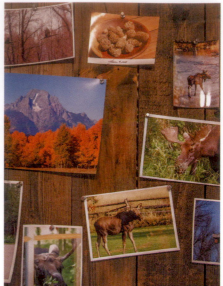

ABOVE Pebbles, rocks, and weathered animal bones were hand-picked by the owner for use as cabinet pulls.

LEFT A modest kitchen is enough to heat a cup of soup or snap open a beer.

CHOOSING YOUR ROOF

Wood shakes, asphalt shingles, and metal panels are the most common roofing materials for cabins. Each has its pros and cons.

Wood can be harvested from renewable forests and damage to the roof can be repaired with a few shingles. However, wood shingles don't offer protection from forest fires or chimney sparks.

Asphalt roofs are inexpensive and can be assembled quickly. The longevity of an asphalt roof is directly dependent on the thickness of the shingles. Asphalt shingles are available in a variety of textures and colors. They should not be used on low-pitched roofs in wind-prone sites as they can be pulled up. They are only slightly better than wood shingles in regard to fire protection.

Metal roofing comes in ribbed or flat sheets and is most commonly fabricated from steel, copper, or zinc that has been galvanized or bonderized. With steel roof sheeting, you also have the option of having a color baked on as a finish. When installing a metal roof, there are several options as to how the sheet can be seamed, most commonly by overlapping clipped ribs (called a standing-seam roof) or by direct face screws with rubber grommets. A metal roof can be expensive; a good candidate would be a simple roof, with no valleys.

Used in snowy regions, metal roofs are prone to snow slides. The snow may sit on the metal roof for several days and then all slide off in one moment, destroying, damaging, or injuring whatever may be below: plants, cars, people, and so on. For that reason, if you choose to use a metal roof in such an area, attention needs to be paid in regard to house design to minimize the possibility that such a slide will cause damage or injury. Clips and bars can be added to standing-seam roofs to significantly reduce snow slides.

Metal roofs offer excellent fire protection, are quite resistant to wind lift, and have considerable longevity. When installed over an insulated roof structure, there is no need to worry about deafening rainstorms.

The original cabin consisted of two A-frames (both still visible),
now expanded upon with the addition of dormer "saddlebags."

"There are woods out there I never saw from the inside before."

"A" PLUS

When designing and building a cabin, it can be hard to anticipate future needs and to plan for them in the initial design. In the case of my clients Bud and Jeannette, it was more than 40 years before they realized their cabin in northern Minnesota needed more space. With four generations now using it as a summer home, the original cabin, designed for one family, needed to accommodate several families and their friends vacationing at the same time. The family also wanted to make it possible to enjoy the cabin year-round. It was time to reinvest and leave a legacy retreat for the generations to come.

The original design, conceived by a friend, architect John Rauma, was a double A-frame structure with three bedrooms, a galley kitchen, a joint living/dining room, one bath, and a loft. Another bedroom and two more baths were needed, and Bud and Jeannette wanted to enlarge the existing bedrooms. They also wanted to increase the size of the kitchen to accommodate a larger dining table, as well as allow two cooks to work at the same time with ease. The interest in year-round use demanded something more than a closet for the new furnace, hot-water heater, and well equipment, as well as more insulation.

Building onto an A-frame can be quite challenging, as the continuity of the rafters spanning from the ridge to the floor is critical. With the help of a structural engineer, we clipped a few rafters in areas where we needed uninterrupted space and in other situations allowed the rafters to fly through the room as a decorative element. I decided to add saddlebag dormers to the A-frame, as doing so retained the A-frame's character while providing the new space where needed.

The windows in the saddlebags direct natural light into the darker areas of the original cabin space and offer views into the surrounding pine forest. New windows were installed to increase the energy efficiency of the cabin, as well as ventilation during the summer.

RIGHT Building a new basement to house the mechanicals was key to expanding the seasons the cabin can be put to use.

BELOW Some of the floor-to-ceiling rafters were cut away in the remodeling but a few remain to carry the structural load (and to provide an interesting decorative element).

After 40 years of use of a cabin they loved, the family approached the new construction with trepidation. But their reactions were positive. "There are woods out there I never saw from the inside before," daughter Lucy said. Daughter Lynn added, "I used to walk around unconsciously listing to one side. Now I can stand erect with ample shoulder room." And mom Jeannette exclaimed, "Oh! This is so right."

ABOVE The original bridge between the two A-frames has been retained in the remodel and remains an important signature feature of the cabin.

ABOVE The original steep ladder stair was replaced with alternating-tread stairs. The addition of rope lighting makes it easier to see the stairs at night.

The original A-frame has a cozy, wood-clad sleeping niche that enjoys a restful view out to the pine forest.

THE A-FRAME

A-frame-shaped dwellings date far back in time and across cultures, but the iconic form familiar to Americans, particularly as cabins, became popular in the 1950s through to the 1970s. The form is easily fabricated from standard milled lumber and can be assembled in just a few weeks, even at remote sites. It is also available in kit packages.

Most of the exterior surface of an A-frame is covered with roofing material and the nonbearing end walls can be fully glazed. Although sizes vary, most are built in increments of 4-ft. rafter length. The width is often large enough so that the midspan structural ties can function as floor joists for a loft. Although striking, the open, angular interior of an A-frame is not the most efficient use of space and is more frequently found in the design of vacation homes rather than primary residences.

ABOVE Architect John Rauma's original concrete and stone fireplace still warms the cabin and makes a nice contrast to fir beams and cedar ceiling.

LEFT Bud's favorite reading chair is in a bay projection in the living room that catches a view down to the lake.

BELOW Nestled in a grove of towering pines, the cabin is a mere stone's throw away from the lake beyond.

This more than century-old living space has been refurbished and restored for the next century.

> "The cabin was built by a rancher and logger, John Hardin, in 1874."

OLD GLORY

In 1923 a group of developers created the Red Feather Mountain Lakes Community 54 miles west of Fort Collins, Colorado, named in honor of Princess Tsianina Redfeather, a world-famous mezzo-soprano of Cherokee and Creek heritage. The area includes over a dozen lakes and is surrounded by 800,000 acres of the Roosevelt National Forest, as well as the towering mountains of Rocky Mountain National Park.

Alex and Ana Bogusky purchased land in the community in 2007, attracted by the wildlife and spectacular scenery just two hours from their home in Boulder. Alex was also smitten by the old log cabin on the property; it was a bit derelict, with some shoddy additions, but it had a solid core. The cabin was built by a rancher and logger, John Hardin, in 1874; Hardin, along with two wives (not at the same time) and nine children would call it home. It is one of the oldest log cabins in northern Colorado.

Alex wanted to renovate the old cabin and hired builder Randy Gillen of Big Horn Custom Builders to tackle the job. Randy stripped away the ramshackle additions and disassembled the logs

The porch shelters arrival and is positioned to catch the sun setting over the Rocky Mountains.

Living room

Kitchen

Porch

0   5   10

for cleaning and sandblasting. The sill logs at the bottom of the walls had rotted, so Randy raised the cabin 2 ft. and set it on a new stone base. The dismantling of the house led to some surprises, like the discovery that there had once been a fire in the attic, as well as a cache of newspapers from 1870 that had been used as insulation.

A new rusted-steel corrugated roof was added to create timeless western character. All the plumbing and wiring inside the cabin was left exposed, transformed into interior details. Old painted cabinets and a classic farmhouse sink added nostalgia to the kitchen, as have a 1930s' refrigerator and a Chambers stove from the 1940s. The original door hardware was reused from the cabin, the latches dated 1898 and the hinges fabricated from ironwork taken from wagon wheels.

Alex is proud of the efforts taken to renovate this 140-year-old structure. He imagines that 140 years hence someone might have to do it again!

ABOVE The Bogusky cabin is surrounded by the 800,000 acres of Roosevelt National Forest in Colorado.

RIGHT New cabinets were made to look timeless and add a sparkle of color to the living space.

MAKING WOOD LAST

Wood can last for many centuries if it is kept dry and free of insects. There are timber structures in Europe that date back several hundred years.

Old log structures can be dismantled by numbering the logs, lifting off the roof, and removing the logs one by one from the top down. Minor log rot can be cleaned away and filled in with cement compound colored to blend in with the weathered wood.

All log structures, new and old, should have roofs with a considerable overhang both at the eaves and gabled ends, and they should be set well off the ground to protect against the incursion of moisture.

TOP/LEFT Plumbing pipes are exposed to minimally impact the old logs of the cabin.

LEFT Different log joinery techniques were employed on two of the cabin's corners, suggesting different builders and a probable addition.

BELOW A tandem bed niche is built into the end of the living space. The ladder leads to a children's sleeping loft above.

A new screened porch (with painted pine floor) shares the lakefront
with a stone terrace.

"Marlene tried to look beyond the cabin's condition to imagine it as it could be."

SUBTRACT AND ADD

Quaint log structures can capture a romantic notion of what cabin life should be, but occasionally their purchase can necessitate substantial reinvestment to meet the expectations of contemporary lifestyles. Century-old structures require updated plumbing, heating, and electrical systems and roofing. Wood rot, undetected under many coats of paint, and foundation settlement may result in doors and windows that won't open and shut properly. And the desire for greater creature comforts may call for bigger bedrooms, nicer baths, and mouse-proof kitchens.

My client Marlene had already experienced decades of bucolic cabin life on a lake in north-central Minnesota, escaping the summer prairie heat of her home in Sioux Falls, South Dakota, a five-hour drive away. Her family cabin was in high demand by a growing enclave of married children, grandchildren, and friends. A few doors away from the family compound, a century-old log cabin came up for sale. She tried to look beyond its current condition to imagine it as it could be. Its dark interior, low ceilings, and tacky additions would have to go, but its real log cabin charm would make this a worthy investment. And she would be just a short stroll away from her grandchildren.

Marlene and I worked together to envision both a subtraction and an addition to create a cabin for the next century. Old lean-tos and a porch were subtracted such that the core "T" log cabin plan was exposed. This structure was then lifted up and a new foundation built underneath it. Rotted sill logs were replaced and two new log courses were added to achieve a reasonable ceiling height. A two-story frame addition was designed, as was a screened porch on the lake side. A new roof joined old and new together.

When all was set back into place, the original log cabin space provided the kitchen/dining area, a main-floor bedroom, a bath,

TOP The original log cabin was enlarged with the addition of a two-story shingled frame structure seen to the left of the house. The garage on the right was also added.

LEFT It was the lake more than anything that encouraged Marlene to drive five hours from South Dakota to northern Minnesota, with thoughts of relaxation on the water.

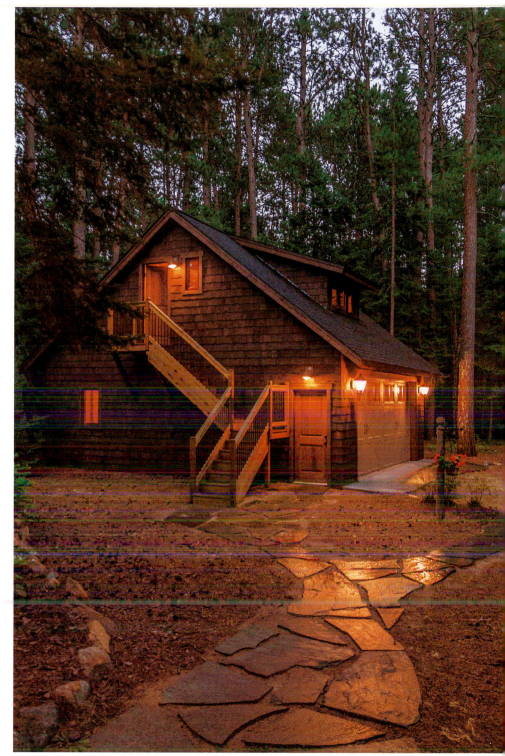

A garage with a sleeping studio above
is snuggled between the trees.

First floor

Screened porch

Living room

Dining

Kitchen

Entry

Bedroom

Office

0   5   10

Second floor

Balcony

Bedroom

Bedroom

and an office alcove. The new space added a gracious entryway and living room, as well as two second-floor bedrooms and a bath. A sliding glass door opens the dining area to the porch. The addition of a skylight and refinishing of the logs lightened up the interior of the kitchen and dining area.

Outside, the addition was finished with milled shingles, a contrasting yet complementary texture to the horizontal logs of the original cabin. A detached garage/workshop with a bunkroom above is now nestled into the pine grove, looking like it has always been there. Both buildings were stained in deep hues of blackish brown to blend with the pine bark and to diminish their scale. But all is not incognito, as friends and family easily find their way to a morning cup of coffee on the porch, a cozy conversation at the fireplace, or a steal-away sleepover with grandmother.

THE CHALLENGES OF LINKING NEW TO OLD

OPPOSITE TOP A small office tucks in behind sliding barn doors in the old log cabin. The original logs were corn blasted to remove layers of varnish without damaging the logs. Modern color-coordinated chinking was applied and the logs were sealed with polyurethane.

OPPOSITE BOTTOM The living room, which is in the addition, shares views of the fireplace (built with regional limestone) and lake. The windows are cottage style, with unequal-size sashes that make it easier to view the water either standing or sitting.

BELOW An evening in the fresh lake air is most enjoyable with the bugs screened out.

Log cabin additions are often best achieved through the use of vertical log or standard frame construction. When cut, tree trunks shrink in diameter, not in length. Thus, horizontal walls of logs shrink accumulatively and can drop 3 in. to 5 in. in the first few years. Old log walls have long since settled, and therefore differential settlement can be a problem at joints and for shared roof construction. This can lead to wind infiltration, water intrusion, or varmint migration.

Contrasting log construction with frame walls can be complementary and add to the variety of cabin surfaces. In the cabin shown here, I employed open-timber beam and decking construction to highlight an alternative use of wood and reduce floor-to-floor heights in the new areas.

Cabins can come as kits delivered on a truck in boxes of parts to be put together or almost entirely prefabricated **PREPACKAGED AND GIFT-WRAPPED** off site. They can also be built from mass-marketed ready-made plans. Which choice works for you will be a function of your site, budget, and aesthetic preferences.

The weeHouse arrived at the site as two boxes, one the single-story portion of the cabin, the other the second-story portion.

> "By summer, everything was shipshape, the cabin finished and outfitted."

INSTANT CABIN

Scott and Lisa McGlasson had vacationed with friends and family on a small northern Minnesota lake just often enough to catch cabin fever. A decade ago they finally found a piece of land they could afford; unfortunately, because the cabin on it was in such irretrievably derelict shape, Scott knew a teardown was in order.

Scott, a furniture builder, had begun his carpentry career by helping architect Geoffrey Warner of Alchemy Architects construct his first weeHouse. Geoff had a client who wanted him to design a small getaway or, as she had put it, "just a wee little house." Geoff built the modular structure in a climate-controlled warehouse, had it trucked to the site, and then hoisted it by crane onto its foundation. Scott had been part of the building team and was sufficiently impressed with the result to contract with Geoff for weeHouse #2, his own cabin by the lake.

The initial weeHouse had been a dry unit, with no budget for a well or septic system. But Scott's parcel had these systems in place, so weeHouse #2 would be bigger than #1, two stories instead of one, with separate bedrooms and a plumbed kitchen and bath.

Geoff designed a cabin that could be built in two modules, each 13 ft. wide, with one 42 ft. long and the other 12 ft. long. Together

LEFT The lake is just a modest drop from the cabin.

BELOW Owner Scott McGlasson designs and builds furniture, including the wheelbarrow table shown here. The living room is made to feel larger by the double opening onto the lake-facing deck.

they could fit on one flatbed truck, a necessity for cost-effective transport. The longer unit would be the main floor and the smaller a second-story bedroom, with an open outdoor stairway to reach it.

Everything was planned for late-fall delivery, but last-minute construction delays pushed the date into winter. Snowdrifts and blistering cold temperatures met the truck and crane at the property. A quick phone call was made to dispatch a snowplow to clear the site. But even with the snow pushed away, the crane, which was costing Scott $300 an hour to rent, was having problems negotiating the site. But by evening, all was in place. Instant cabin…almost!

Scott still had to button up the joints of the two modules, hook up the plumbing and electrical, and do some interior trim work, which he did through the spring months. By summer, everything was shipshape, the cabin finished and outfitted, waiting only for dishes, linen, and his own handcrafted furniture.

Several seasons have passed since the cabin was completed, and Scott, family, and friends have amassed a rich array of memories, from bonfires, fishing, and swimming to quiet times spent reading a book or gazing up at the stars. It may be a weeHouse, but they are not wee experiences.

Box dwellings are narrow, so the galley kitchen also serves as corridor to the main-floor bedroom.

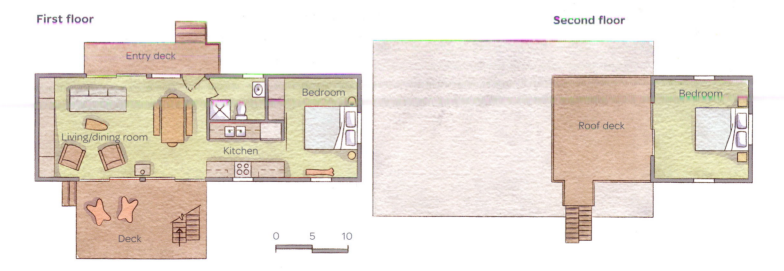

First floor

Entry deck

Bedroom

Living/dining room

Kitchen

Deck

0   5   10

Second floor

Roof deck

Bedroom

LOAD LIMITS

Prefab modular units have one thing in common: the load limitations of transport on federal, state, and local highways. Weight is rarely an issue, but dimensions are. Width, height, and length limits vary across states and types of roads, but commonly these are 14 ft., 13 ft. including the wheels, and 60 ft., respectively.

Sites have to be accessible to a big flatbed truck and a large crane. Modular units must be designed not only to carry local snow and wind loads but also the unique torque load of being hoisted by a crane.

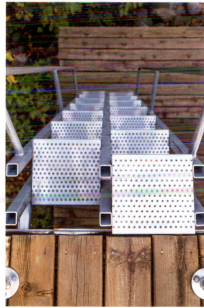

ABOVE A deck extends the living space outside. The metal staircase provides access to the second-story bedroom.

LEFT The alternating tread stair was fabricated by the owner.

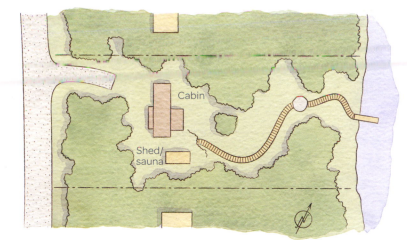

Cabin

Shed/
sauna

The Carolina Jessamine Cottage was a model house at Camp Calloway in Georgia when the owners bought it. It can be built from purchased plans.

"At night we love to open the door to the screened porch so we can hear the chorus of frogs singing."

GEORGIA PEACH

Camp Callaway is a neighborhood of cabins nestled into the trees along Martin Lake, located near Pine Mountain, Georgia. An hour southwest of Atlanta, it's a bucolic area of rolling hills, reservoirs, and streams, a popular destination for water sports, hunting, fishing, and summer youth camps. Camp Callaway is also part of the 4,600-acre Callaway Gardens preserve, which is committed to land stewardship, ecological research, and greater appreciation of the natural world.

The camp offers buyers a choice of four cabin designs; all of them are designed to EarthCraft Standards, a green building certification program used in six southeastern states. The cabins utilize geothermal heating and cooling and are designed to blend into their wooded environment, with no manicured lawns.

Tanya Andoniadis had attended camp at Callaway with a cousin for two years when she was 8 and 9 years old. In 2003 and the summers that followed, she returned to the area with her husband, Matthew, and children in tow. In 2010 she and her husband discovered Camp Callaway on a bike ride and toured its four models.

A compact living area brings family and guests together. The painted wood paneling creates an open, fresh appearance (below), while the kitchen bar serves as a subtle divider between food preparation and living space (above).

Kevin Clark of Historical Concepts designed prototypes for the development to capture distinct vernacular forms, "with a goal of having very quaint quarters, fitted out in detail, and tucked within the wooded property."

"We loved the concept so much that we almost decided to purchase a lot," Tanya notes. However, she struggled with the prospect of having to decorate and furnish their to-be-built vacation home from more than 800 miles away. That problem was solved when, a month later, one of the model homes, the Carolina Jessamine Cottage, was put on the market, fully furnished. A deal was made.

According to Kevin, for this particular model, "A key 'ingredient' was the use of wood throughout the home in lieu of drywall. This allowed for the 'cabin' character to continue in from the outside." In the tradition of Southern rural cottages, the wood is painted inside and out. The muddy red palette of the exterior, the color of Georgia clay, is used to soften the home's appearance in the trees. Inside the cottage, a variety of lighter shades is utilized to bounce around the dappled light.

First floor

Screened porch

Bedroom

Living room

Kitchen

Bedroom

Powder room

Entry

Stoop

Second floor

Bunkroom

Sitting room

0   5   10

The porch is generously deep, with ample space for alfresco dining, and the use of a wire railing system instead of wooden rails and spindles results in a more open feel. On hot summer nights in any climate, an outdoor ceiling fan provides a welcome breeze.

"From the moment we walked into our new home, we were able to enjoy it. At night we love to open the door to the screened porch so we can hear the chorus of frogs singing. It's truly a home where our family sits back and relaxes and enjoys each other's company," Tanya exclaims. The Andoniadises purposely did not equip the cabin with cable, Internet, or phone. "This forces us to put our feet up and enjoy a good book and prompts the kids to find their own fun by rediscovering nature and playing outside."

CABIN COMMUNITY

Parking

Golf-cart path

Cabin

A cozy sleeping area is built into the roof upstairs. It can be closed off from an adjoining sitting room by sliding doors. The beds are built in, with storage below and bookcases as headboards. Color on the floors, walls, and cabinets adds a lively exuberance to this space.

MODEL CABINS

Many Americans prefer to make their purchases "off the rack" so they can "kick the tires" and don't have to wait for a custom model to be built for them. For this sort of experience when shopping for a vacation home, look for large-development, second-home communities. These tend to be located within a few hours' drive of metropolitan areas where greater market demand can make the builder's spec costs of buying the land, creating the necessary infrastructure, and building the model homes financially viable.

Ready-made models carry the benefit of known costs. When making your purchase from some distance away, this can provide a great deal of security.

The model unit that Matthew and Tanya Andoniadis bought at Camp Callaway was sponsored by *Southern Living* magazine and built by Pine Mountain Development. The prototype plan, Carolina Jessamine Cottage, is available through the magazine.

ABOVE Two main-floor bedrooms are a feature of this stock plan, which makes the most of its small spaces (here, using a sliding door to access the bathroom).

RIGHT The cabin looks out over an arm of Lake Martin, and although it's part of a tightly clustered development, there is a sense of solitude because of the efforts that were taken to retain as many trees as possible when building.

"After an evening of camaraderie, they climbed into their container cabin for a good night's rest."

THE WELL-CONTAIN(ER)ED CABIN

For years, brothers Paul and Scott Stankey had enjoyed visiting their family's vacation property two hours north of Minneapolis, most recently taking shelter there in a decrepit trailer they shared with an abundance of mice. When the time finally came to consider a more permanent structure, Scott, a builder, and Paul, an architect, along with Paul's then fiancée, Sarah Nordby (also an architect), sat down to examine their options.

With budgetary considerations in mind and taking the trailer as a jumping off point, they landed on the mother of all repurposed receptacles: the shipping container. Used to move freight across the globe via train and boat, these metal boxes are 8 ft. wide, 8 ft. 6 in. tall, and 20 ft. or 40 ft. long. Made of corten steel, they are commonly decommissioned after a decade of heavy use. What better reuse of these world travelers than as a cabin in the woods? Paul began sketching design concepts based on the steel behemoths, while Scott went hunting for two retired containers.

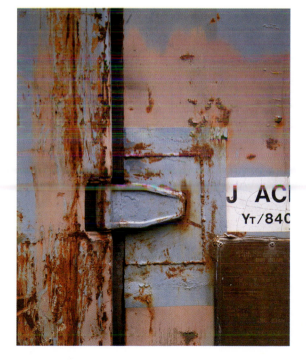

OPPOSITE Two shipping containers have been parked in the forest with a glass atrium built between. The end doors on the containers open to reveal windows for light and ventilation.

Stoop

Dining room

Kitchen

Living room

Sleeping

Deck

0   5   10

The center atrium serves as the dining area and as a light source to each container through openings cut in to their side walls. The atrium opens to a sunny south-facing deck.

A cache was soon found in Minneapolis and the price was right: $800 per 20-ft.-long box. It took a pickup truck, two trips, and one very long day to move the 5,000-lb. containers to their site near a trout stream. It has taken another several years and many weekends to hoist the containers onto foundations, cut openings in the sides, build a glass-framed link between them, insulate, trim out the interior with paneling and cabinets, and insert a wood-stove. But each year brings a little more refinement, most recently a sun deck. Somewhere in the future there exists the prospect of solar power, a fresh-water well, and, just maybe, a bathroom.

Their weekends at the retreat aren't entirely devoted to labor. There is time to cross-country ski, fish, hunt, and take exploratory hikes over the rest of the family's forested acreage. They recently put their fire pit to use for a pig roast that was savored by friends and family. After an evening of camaraderie, they climbed into their container cabin for a good night's rest.

RECYCLING CONTAINERS

Discarded shipping containers have been put to use in a plethora of ways throughout the world, best recorded in the 2010 book *Container Atlas: A Practical Guide to Container Architecture*.

When these containers are used for habitation, there are unique issues associated with their insulation, the insertion of windows, and outfitting them with electricity and plumbing. The containers do provide instant shelter, so they are an attractive option for the do-it-yourselfer. Although exceptionally stout and strong, shipping containers repurposed in this way are a challenge for building codes and may be a better option in areas where codes are more lax.

ABOVE The living room with its woodstove is in the west container, accessed through two openings cut into its side wall.

A portion of the east container has been turned into the kitchen. A sleeping loft is perched above.

TOP/BOTTOM LEFT The Stankey family property is dotted with mobile dwellings large and small.

BELOW Even a simple storage shed for outdoor toys can look stylish.

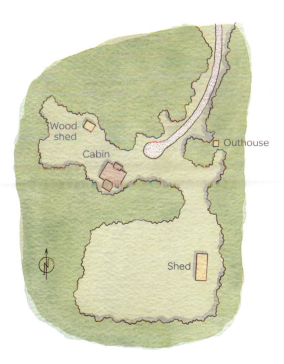

The extended Stankey family has had a long history with portable buildings (trailers, pop-up tents, RVs, and more trailers) on this property, so the containers fit right in. Paul thinks their containers are roomy and airy compared to earlier trailer experiences. As to why containers and not mobile homes this time, Scott answered, "I appreciate a different approach, one that offers the tactile pleasure of unlocking and opening the boxes' big swinging metal doors." Plus, he says, "There's the history of these boxes having traveled the world carrying only God knows what. There is a unique mystery to them that you do not get from a bunch of two-by-fours."

> "The light moves through the house over the course of the day, a precious commodity during the gray days of the Puget Sound."

HOME RUN

Some architects create prototype home plans on speculation, seeking to conceive designs with mass-market appeal. In the case of Ross Chapin and his company, Good Fit, he works backward from that, designing for clients and making plans available for wider purchase only if he feels the design is one that will work uncoupled from the specific requirements of the original site (and, of course, if the original client gives their permission).

Just such a case are the plans Chapin drew up for a 635-sq.-ft. guest cottage on Whidbey Island near Seattle, Washington, for Gil and Ann Graham. The property the Grahams purchased had a modest cabin on it that Chapin had designed for the previous owner. The couple intended to retire there and sought Chapin's counsel for adding to the structure.

LEFT The cottage is positioned on an open knoll with a south-facing terrace.

OPPOSITE A built-in window seat provides extra seating in the small living room and is a great place to snuggle up with a book.

TOP Two pairs of French doors open to the terrace of
the guest cottage with a view back to the Grahams'
primary home.

ABOVE The site of the Gilann Cottage has a spectacular
view of Puget Sound and the shipping lane.

The Grahams and Chapin decided that the best strategy for
satisfying their needs was to build a small addition onto the
existing cabin; this would become their residence. To accommodate
visitors, a guest cottage/studio with two bedrooms and communal
living space would be built at the back of the property. The
Grahams knew that a number of their regular visitors would be
elderly, and asked that the structure be kept to a single story.
They also asked Chapin to design the guest house so that it would
look as if it had been built at the same time as the primary
structure, using the same style of windows and the same paint
color, and erecting a lattice shelter over the guest house patio.
Chapin also added his signature built-ins throughout the house—

The ladder gives access to a sleeping loft above. A linen cabinet terminates the short hall.

including a window seat in the living room, drawers in one of the bedrooms, and a kitchenette—making the most of the available space and creating a welcome ambiance of coziness.

"Ross hit a home run," enthuses Ann Graham. "The guest cottage seems so much bigger than its actual square footage." She loves the way it sits on the property and "how the views from each room add to a feeling of contentment." The light moves through the house over the course of the day, a precious commodity during the gray days of the Puget Sound.

The positive feedback Chapin received from the Grahams and their guests suggested to him that others might want to utilize this plan. In honor of the Grahams, he named the plan Gilann Cottage, and promised not to sell it anywhere in the vicinity of Whidbey Island.

LEFT As a guest cabin, there's no need for a stovetop in the compact kitchenette. The microwave, under-counter refrigerator, and sink are sufficient for preparing snacks and small meals.

OPPOSITE BOTTOM In lieu of a closet, a niche provides a bench for suitcases and hooks for clothing.

PREPACKAGED COTTAGE AND CABIN PLANS

There are several companies that sell cabin and cottage plans, ready for the building. In addition to Chapin's Good Fit Company on the West Coast, there is Robert Knight's Lucia's Little Houses, which offers an excellent array of plans generated from actual projects in New England. *Southern Living* House Plans has several cabin plans under 1,000 sq. ft., such as Deer Run, a two-bedroom, two-bath gable structure with a porch, metal roof, and board-and-batten siding.

Plans can also be found in the back pages of many cabin and cottage magazines. They can be ordered as study plans for a modest cost, or you can purchase multiple sets of construction drawings ready for bidding by your contractor. Plans created for generic use should be reviewed by an architect or engineer in the area you intend to build so local conditions—soil, zoning, building codes—as well as available materials can be accounted for.

> "Set in a clearing in the forest, complete with a campfire area for bonfires, sing-alongs, and cookouts."

THE HAMLET

Terry Anderson, along with St. Paul neighbor Sarah Stonich (see p. 144), had found acreage near the Boundary Waters Canoe Area along the Canadian border. The land was accessed by an old logging trail and fronted a pastoral spring-fed lake. The rocky terrain discouraged investing in the drilling of a well, and the remoteness of the property made electrical hook-up prohibitively expensive. A low-cost, low-tech solution seemed the most appropriate choice in light of the conditions.

Terry envisioned a modest cabin, outhouse, workshop, and guest house/sauna, which would function as a substitute for a shower. He turned to Eric Mase, who lived just down the logging trail, for help. Eric and his wife, Dayna, had built a diminutive cabin on their site, just the kind of low-impact, environmentally sensitive approach Terry was looking for.

Eric had developed a particular method of timber framing when building his cabin, predominantly using 6-in. by 6-in. spruce

LEFT This wilderness setting is home to a hamlet of small structures nestled among the trees.

OPPOSITE The main cabin was set on piers so as to minimize cutting into tree roots, as well as to preserve the intimate forest setting. The deck faces east, overlooking a spring-fed lake.

The modest 12-ft. by 18-ft. space is still large enough to accommodate the kitchen, eating area, living room, and a sleeping loft above. The ladder rolls out of the way when not in use.

lumber for the posts, beams, braces, and rafters. The posts rest on low-impact concrete pier footings. The framing is filled in with a 2×4 insulated wall and sheathed inside and out with pine siding. The insulated roof is capped in ribbed metal sheets.

Most timber framers fabricate all the parts of the frame at their shop, whereas Eric builds them on site, including the roof, which he builds on the ground and then has lifted into place by a crane. When all is completed, these structures feel as if they were lovingly lowered from a helicopter, perfectly nestled into place.

Cabin

Kitchen

Living

Deck

Outhouse

Guest/sauna

Sauna

Guest

Shop

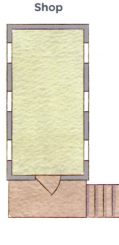

0   5   10

Terry's main cabin is 12 ft. by 18 ft., with a kitchen, eating area, sofa, and sleeping loft. A library ladder gives access to the loft and can be rolled out of the way during the day. The space is heated with a woodstove and propane is used for cooking. A lookout deck fronts the cabin, offering views to the lake.

The main cabin was completed in the spring of 2006; that summer the shop was built. The roof is fitted with south-facing solar panels, which generate the electricity he needs for his woodworking equipment.

The roof of the workshop is fitted with solar panels, which generate enough electricity to power Terry's woodworking equipment as well as lights for the hamlet.

Being off the grid, a sauna offers an
opportunity for relaxing as well as
cleaning up.

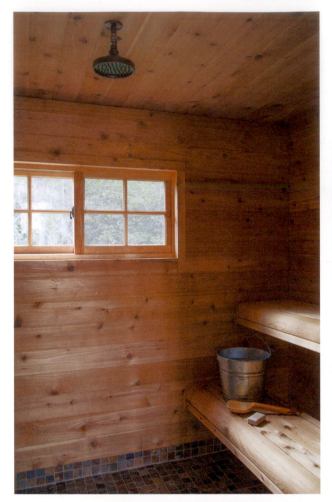

Begun in 2007, the guest house/sauna is near completion.
Collectively, these structures will form what Terry likes to call The
Hamlet, set in a clearing in the forest, complete with a campfire
area for bonfires, sing-alongs, and cookouts. "My vision has been to
ultimately recreate the feel of a mom-and-pop resort, with perhaps
a couple more small cabins added so friends can stay for extended
periods of time," says Terry.

Even the outhouse is a
timberframe structure.

THOREAU NORTH

Eric Mase left Chicago for a quiet life in Minnesota's north woods, earning his living by working at a resort and building birchbark canoes. Within a few years he married Dayna, bought land, and started searching for a way to build a modest structure that could make use of his carpentry skills. In a book on shed construction he discovered timber framing. Together, he and Dayna built "Thoreau," a 10-ft. by 15-ft. timber structure. They began construction using the cordwood technique (kind of like stacking firewood, with the cut ends facing out), but slow progress in a bug-infested environment suggested that they switch to 2x4 standard stud construction between the timber frame and windows. Upon viewing the completed cabin, a guest noted it was a "wee little cabin" and a business was born, Wee Cabin Company. Eric offers three designs for what he calls "storybook" style Wee Cabins.

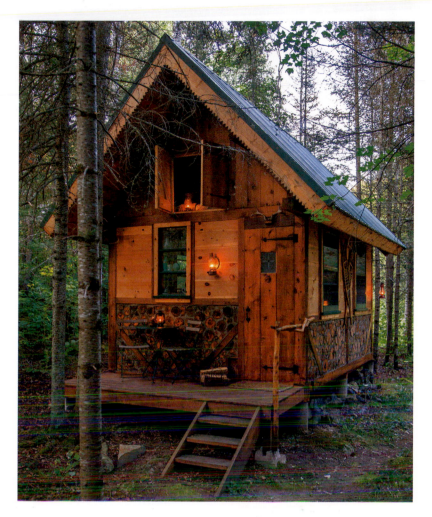

It was this small house Eric Mase built for himself that inspired Terry to ask him to design and construct a hamlet of his own Wee Cabins. Called "Thoreau", Eric's cabin is a timberframe and cordwood structure.

> "This unit arrives on site as a kit ready for you or your building crew to put together."

A KERNEL IDEA

Log cabin prototypes can be seen by the side of the road in cabin country and at log-home-building trade shows, and their plans are sold in the back of log-building trade or home design magazines. The same is true of "A-frames," timberframe cabins, and stud-frame prototypes.

Many prototypes started life as a project for a specific client and site. Such is the case with The Crib by architect Jeffrey Broadhurst. The original client wanted a getaway to replace a derelict fishing cottage set on a riverbank. The design needed to work within the existing small footprint. Jeff's search for a solution to maximize interior space led him to the idea of canting the walls out over the footprint, reminiscent of the corn crib (see "Corn Cribs" on p. 140).

The client lost interest in the project, but the idea of a small house based on the form of the corn crib continued to percolate in Jeff's mind. Eventually he followed through on his initial

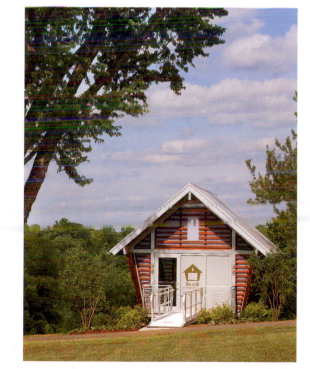

LEFT On the entry side, a narrow bridge provides access. The roof is galvanized steel.

OPPOSITE The Crib is temporarily sited at an art center, convenient for public viewing. It's designed to sit atop four footings.

A "kitchen in a box" that closes into a cabinet when not in use fits under the sleeping loft. The living space balloons in the middle to make a tiny footprint feel larger.

inspiration, developing prototype plans for three sizes of The Crib: the Basic Crib, with 175 sq. ft.; the Full Crib at 250 sq. ft.; and, finally, a grand and elaborate Extended Crib with 390 sq. ft., including a kitchen and bathroom. Each comes with an outdoor deck to extend the living space and offers possible upgrades, like screen panels, a woodstove, a loft, a kitchen in a box, and more.

Unlike the weeHouse prototype (see p. 106) that comes pre-assembled, this unit arrives on site as a kit ready for you or your building crew to put together. "The assembly process requires the use of a small crane or boom tractor and two or three skilled builders," says Jeff's promotional literature. He suggests it might take two to three weeks to assemble, assuming the foundation piers are already in.

The view from the loft highlights the flexible living/dining space. A glass garage door opens to provide access to the balcony.

CORN CRIBS

Utilitarian and agrarian buildings have often been the source for designer inspiration. The shed, the barn, the silo, and the garage have all found their way into cabin designs. The 19th- and 20th-century corn crib has recently taken center stage as a form worthy of exploration for habitable space.

This form was developed to expedite the drying of cob corn. Its canted side walls were meant to shield the harvested corn from the rain. The horizontal slats allowed air to flow. They were commonly erected as two parallel cribs (sheltered by a single roof) with either an air slit between or a gap that would allow a wagon or truck to drive through.

The form of the corn crib recommends itself for use in home design because it can create a light-filled space with the perception of privacy. It's also an easy structure to fabricate and erect.

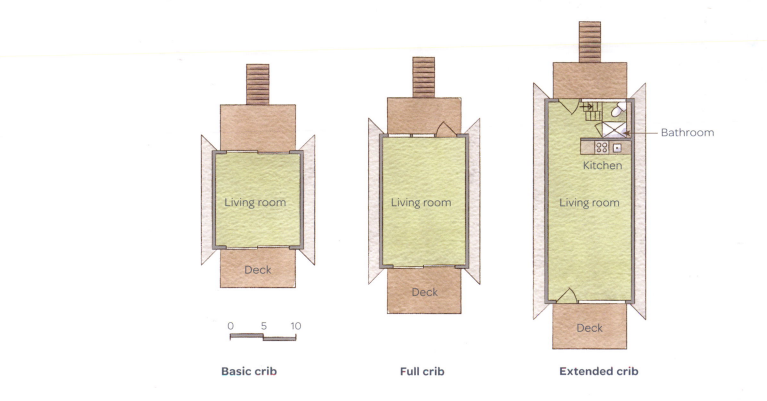

Basic crib **Full crib** **Extended crib**

0   5   10

Bathroom

Kitchen

Living room

Living room

Living room

Deck

Deck

Deck

A propane-fired stove (with slate surround) provides heat. The walls of The Crib are translucent polycarbonate panels that glow with natural light; diagonal bracing keeps the frame from racking.

After developing the plans for The Crib, Jeff realized he needed to put it in front of the public. Americans are a pragmatic lot, and being able to "kick the tires" of a house you think you might want to buy is still a preferred method of house hunting. He approached the Strathmore Arts Center in Bethesda, Maryland, and to his surprise received an enthusiastic response to his proposal of having The Crib set in their sculpture garden for a few years. In 2011 it was installed and has since won awards from *Custom Home* magazine and the Potomac Valley Chapter of the AIA.

Cabins have in the past, and continue today, to exhibit environmentally friendly ideas. Recycled local materials and **STEP LIGHTLY ON THE EARTH** low energy consumption serve to make the cabin green. But the greatest green factor comes in sensitivity to the site and its surroundings — the forest, shoreline, and mountains and the creatures that call these places home.

Log cabin builder Mark Johnson constructed a rustic traditional
scribed log cabin for author Sarah Stonich.

"Four modest structures set into the bucolic landscape for Sarah, her son, and friends to enjoy."

STORY LINE

Cabins have often been central to an author's tale, such as in Thoreau's *Walden*, *Uncle Tom's Cabin* by Harriet Beecher Stowe, and Helen Hoover's *A Place in the Woods*. A recent addition to the genre is Sarah Stonich's chronicle of her cabin-building experience, *Shelter*. In it she reminisces about cabin days with her father and tells how she sought to replicate that experience for her own son. Since her family place had long been sold, she records the story of her own land purchase in northern Minnesota.

After a considerable search to find a plot of remote land that she could afford, Sarah buys acreage on a small lake located near the Boundary Waters Canoe Area separating the United States from Canada. It takes three years to begin construction, with builder and sawmill owner Mark Johnson, and her finances limit Sarah to a modest 10-ft. by 12-ft. uninsulated/unheated log structure. It is fabricated in Johnson's log yard, then dismantled and reassembled on Sarah's site, where it is left through the winter as an open frame to settle and gray out the wood. The following year a roof, windows, and door are added. Along the way, an outhouse is constructed.

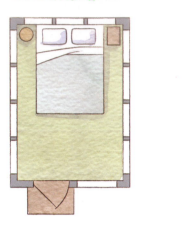

Guest sleeping cabin

Main cabin

ABOVE This structure was originally meant to be a utility building but was repurposed as a sleeping cabin before it was completed.

BELOW Porch sleeping requires mosquito netting to ensure a sound rest. A copy of Stonich's book is available for guests to peruse.

0   5   10

The smallness of the cabin, even with a loft, soon results in a bad case of cabin fever. Just a year after its construction, work begins on a storage shed. Frequent summer guests make it necessary to transform the 8-ft. by 12-ft. shed into a guest cabin before it is even completed. Once the guest house is finished, construction begins on the storage shed, this time equipped with a solar roof.

Sarah's tale ends six years after the initial land purchase, with four modest structures set into the bucolic landscape for Sarah, her son, and friends to enjoy. But a sequel may be on the horizon, as her dreams for a proper kitchen and bathroom in a cabin she can use year round portend new chapters to come.

TOP Even a 10-ft. by 12-ft. cabin can have a place to prepare tea and biscuits for breakfast.

LEFT Because there is no sink in the cabin, activities like dishwashing and shaving are best done outdoors.

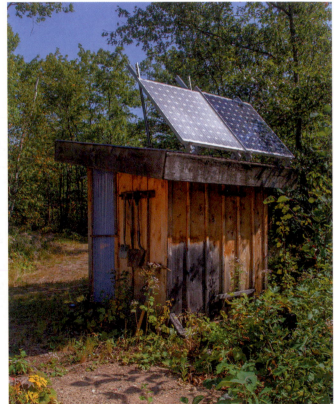

LEFT A pretty privy hides in the woods, adding tranquility to necessity.

BELOW A limited amount of power is generated from solar panels to run a few lights, a radio, or recharge the computer.

THE ENDURING WONDER OF WALDEN

No one book captures the cabin imagination more than Henry David Thoreau's *Walden*. It continues to be widely quoted, has many a cabin named after it, and is preserved as a historic icon in Concord, Massachusetts.

Thoreau began its construction in 1845 on the shore of Walden Pond. Just 10 ft. by 15 ft., with a root cellar and an attic, it is a modest place. Walden was part of an experiment in independent living, where Thoreau stayed for two years, living off the land and detailing his methods, his materials, and their costs.

Although in the woods, Thoreau wasn't totally isolated, and said of visitors, "I had three chairs in my house; one for solitude, two for friendship, three for society. When the visitors came in larger and unexpected numbers there was but the third chair for them all, but they generally economized the room by standing up. It's surprising how many great men and women a small house will contain."

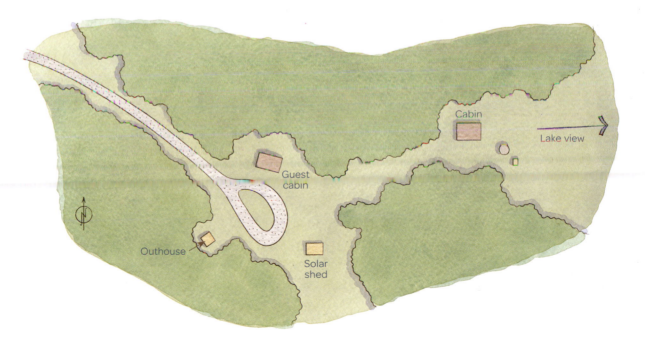

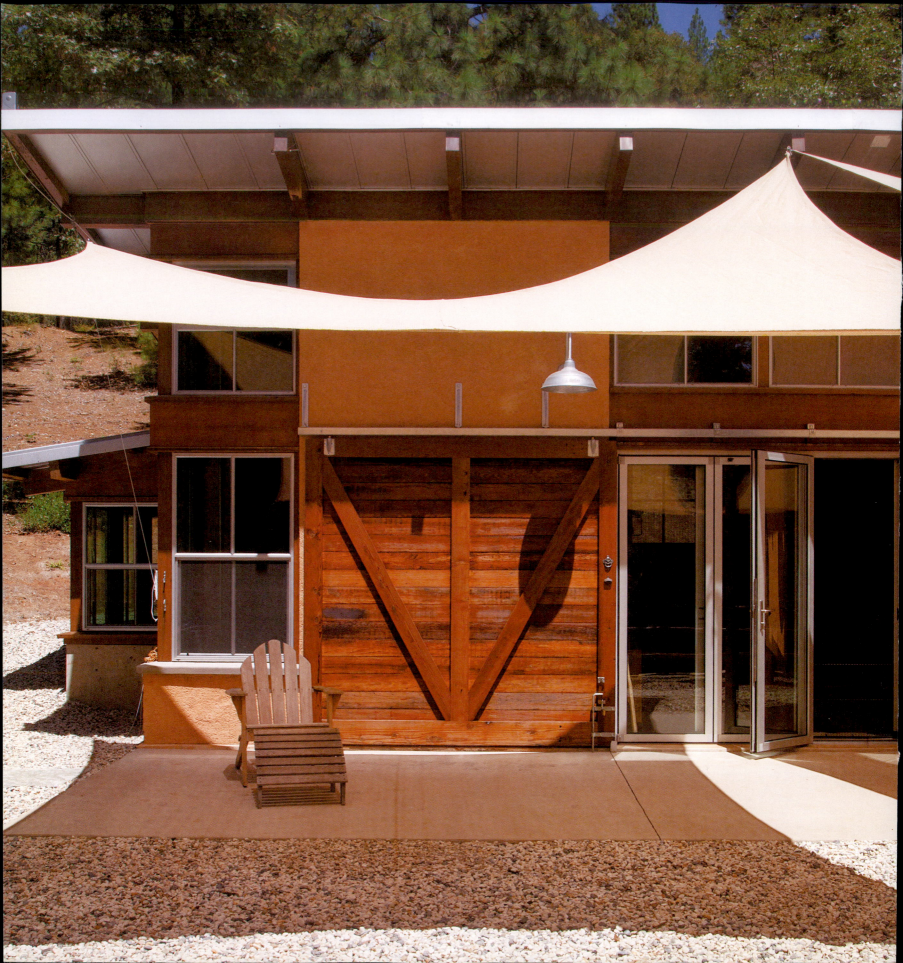

"The smaller entry shed has a south-facing roof equipped with photovoltaic panels."

ENERGY SHED

For their two sons and many friends, the family cabin in the foothills of the Sierra Nevada Mountains is a veritable clubhouse, with zip lines, forts, mountain biking, and bows and arrows. For the parents, it is an environmentally sensitive retreat just a three-hour drive from their home in San Francisco, a place where they can bask in solitude as well as enjoy the work of restoring the ponderosa pine and oak forest on the 44-acre property.

The couple bought the property a decade ago. Its wilderness location necessitated that they be "off the grid." Because of this, the cabin needed to be set in a clearing to allow for solar access. This was also important to protect the cabin against the possibility of forest fire, as was building the structure to be as noncombustible as possible.

The father had taken classes at the Solar Institute in California, where he met architect David Arkin. He was impressed with Arkin's focus on sustainable buildings and hired Arkin and his partner, Annie Tilt, to design a modest cabin that met all these challenges.

LEFT A rustic road is the only access to this remote retreat deep in the forest of Northern California.

OPPOSITE A shade sail anchored to the house and the trees far beyond keeps the summer sun from overheating the cabin. It is taken down in the winter.

LEFT The cabin is located at the north edge of a clearing to fully access the sunlight coming over the tall pines.

BELOW The cabin is constructed of straw bales, which are clad in stucco on the exterior for fire resistance. You can see the solar panels that heat the cabin's water to the right. The gravel perimeter is an important feature in protecting the house in case of a forest fire.

RIGHT This built-in queen-size bed takes the window seat to its luxurious, logical conclusion. Why curl up with a book on a couple of pillows when you can have an entire bed?

BELOW The end of the plastered-over thick straw-bale wall is highlighted at the entry.

Entry

Living room

Bed

Kitchen

Solar panels

Terrace

0 5 10

What they came up with is a 20-ft. by 30-ft. straw-bale shed with two stud-frame extensions, a larger one housing the bathroom, the cabin's mechanical systems, and the entry, and the other for a built-in queen-size bed. The shed contains the dining and communal living space, as well as a kitchen that is tucked under a sleeping loft.

For fire protection, stucco has been applied to the straw bales (see "Straw Bale 101" on p. 154) and the extensions are clad with cement siding. The cabin is capped with a standing-seam metal roof, providing added fire protection and low maintenance.

Several energy-capturing strategies were employed in the cabin. The smaller entry shed has a south-facing roof equipped with photovoltaic panels. These panels harvest energy, which is stored in batteries in a mechanical shed up the hill from the cabin. The electricity they generate is used to power the well pump, lights, and refrigerator.

RIGHT The large solar panels on the ground are for hot water production. The photovoltaic panels on the roof generate electricity for the house and have battery storage attached. Propane gas fuels a backup generator if needed and the cooking stove.

BELOW The bathroom is accessible from inside and out.

Adjacent to the mechanical room in the cabin there are solar hot water collectors. The larger straw-bale shed features south-facing windows for passive solar gain. The windows throughout the cabin were positioned to maximize cross-ventilation when opened.

There is a large storage tank that can hold a reserve of water pumped up from the well to tide the family over if there is an extended run of cloudy days or to use as fire protection, or they can keep the electricity flowing by using a gas-fired generator.

The family is justifiably proud of their energy-producing retreat.

STRAW BALE 101

We eat massive amounts of grain products in America and a by-product of grain production is straw. This can be recycled in the field or baled to be used for animal bedding or made available for construction. Straw-bale homes are energy efficient, have great soundproofing qualities, and are an excellent choice for do-it-yourself homebuilders.

Straw-bale walls are created by stacking 16-in.- to 22-in.-square bales on a raised concrete foundation (at least 12 in. high to prevent moisture intrusion from the ground). Wood frames are set into the bale walls for doors and windows. An extended wood plate caps each straw wall, providing perfectly level tops to set roof trusses on. It's best to choose a roofing system that distributes the load equally across the walls rather than concentrating it on a few locations.

The walls are finished on the outside with lath and stucco and on the inside with lath and plaster. It's key that the bales contain very little moisture before being sealed in stucco and plaster, or they will begin to rot after time. Because of the very real challenge of trying to build a straw-bale house without having its dryness compromised by rain before it has been clad in its protective stucco and plaster, this type of construction is best suited for dry climates, like Utah, New Mexico, Arizona, and Colorado.

The kitchen catches the morning sunlight and has a sleeping loft above. The concrete floor is heated by the solar-panel system.

155

The cabin is built into a western-facing riverbank and has an earthen roof. The exposed walls have an abundance of south-, west-, and north-facing windows, filling the cabin with natural light.

"There was little money left for furniture, so they built the furnishings themselves."

EARTH AND SKY

In 1940, Professor Joseph Beach and his wife, Dagmar, hired their architect friends, Elizabeth (Lisl) Close and her husband, Winston, to design a cabin on a tract of land they had purchased on the bank of the St. Croix River in Wisconsin. The Beaches were about to embark on a sabbatical that would take them out of the region for a year. Trusting their friends to fulfill their vision for the cabin, they handed over what was a pot of money at the time, $1,200, to cover the cost of the plans and construction of the cabin, as well as some modest furnishings. And then they left.

The Closes took up the challenge, testing various design ideas for the steep hillside conditions. They settled on a scheme that recessed the cabin into the hill, with the back stone wall of the house, inset with a fireplace, functioning as a retaining wall. Realizing that any earth removal up the embankment would require significant labor and cost, the Closes made a negative a positive: The cabin would have an earthen roof. They had seen such dwellings in rural Norway and liked the idea of essentially a hidden structure; approaching it from above, one would see only hillside. And a chimney.

The outward-facing western wall was designed with French doors and windows, providing views to the river valley below and access to the terrace immediately outside.

ABOVE When approaching the site, the first reference to the cabin is a chimney protruding from the earth.

BELOW The back retaining wall and fireplace are built of local limestone. The beams and decking overhead have been engineered to carry the weight of wet earth.

Initially there was no electricity brought onto the site and thus no well for water. Bathing consisted of swimming in the river, and an outhouse was built a brief downwind walk away from the cabin. Refrigeration took the form of a large metal can dug into the hillside.

"The cabin had no water supply except for a running brook nearby. The only way to get water was for Joseph to meander down to the brook and bring up a pail full, one at a time. It was primitive in many ways," noted Lisl, who was Minnesota's first modern architect as well as its first woman architect.

As the Closes neared completion of the project, there was little money left for furniture, so they built the furnishings themselves. From plywood and clothesline, they fabricated chairs, a table, a sofa, and a bed.

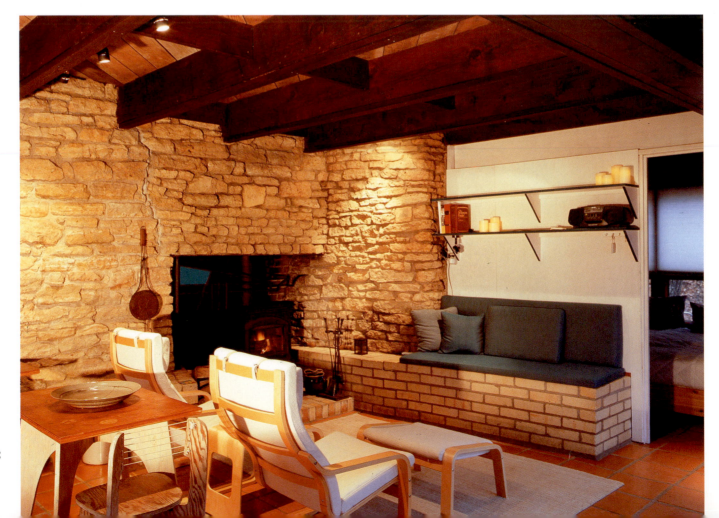

The inset in the wall that now holds a wine rack once housed a metal garbage can that served as a sort of icebox.

Terrace

Bedroom

Living room

Kitchen

Tree house

Screened porch

Bedroom

Living room

0   5   10

The woodstove set in the fireplace provides more efficient heating of the cabin. The metal arm to the left of the fireplace was designed to swing a popcorn rack into the flames.

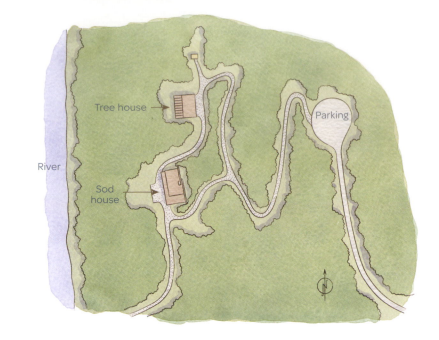

ABOVE Designed by the Closes, the table and chair were made from a single sheet of plywood. The backrest is clothesline.

RIGHT Twenty years after the Sod House was built, the Tree House was added for guests and a different sort of fresh-air experience. It contains a kitchen, sitting area, bath, and bedroom and is fronted by a sizeable screened porch.

The porch of the Tree House originally had a screen roof, which has been replaced with translucent panels that provide some protection from rain.

HEAVENLY EARTH

Earthen-roofed houses have a rich history in Scandinavia and other cultures. When the proper site conditions exist, earth can be used as an insulator, keeping a cabin cooler in the summer and warmer in the winter.

Proper moisture protection, such as the use of a rubber membrane, is important for ensuring a dry living space. Appropriate structural support is also crucial, as wet (and snow-covered) earth is extremely heavy; this should be calculated by an architect or engineer. Last, earthen roofs should support only green pasture; planting them with shrubs or trees will add weight as well as the potential of invasive roots compromising the roof membrane.

When the Beaches returned, they were enraptured with their getaway and regularly invited the Close family to stay with them there. Twenty years later, after Joseph's death, Dagmar commissioned Winston and Lisl to design a tree-house-like structure for visiting guests. The tree house is in direct contrast to the earthen-roofed house: open and airy, with screen walls and roof. Electricity and plumbing were added to the guesthouse and sod house at this time.

The friendship between the families extended for many more years. In 1985, the Close family bought the dwelling from the next generation of the Beach family and today it is owned by son Roy Close and his wife, Linda. They have replaced the rolled roofing under the sod with a rubber membrane and restored the terrace. The rusted metal refrigeration can has given way to a plastic one, but the Sod House and Tree House, as Lisl christened them, remain intact as a family retreat along the river.

Whether sitting on the porch or at the fire pit, the cabin experience can be most spectacular at night in locations with a big sky dome and an unending horizon.

"A tiny space that's as well insulated as a thermos bottle."

CABIN CLASSROOM

Cabins are often the focus of architectural design studio classes, as they present most all of the issues common to designing a building, but on a modest scale, one more easily grasped by students new to the topic.

Recent cabin studios at North Carolina State University and the University of Minnesota have produced imaginative and inventive designs that have been reproduced in the pages of *Cabin Life* magazine, while students at Texas Tech University were challenged to design and build a sustainable, off-the-grid cabin. Their hard work, led by Professor Urs Peter Flueckiger, resulted in an AIA-Texas Merit Award in 2011. More important, it gave students first-hand experience in testing design theory against the real world.

Over three successive semesters, classes at Texas Tech built the energy-efficient structure in a warehouse on campus. They began the project by dismantling a four-axle steel trailer chassis, and then reassembled it to provide the framing for their cabin. Its unique bellows shape allows for enhanced viewing of the prairie and the night sky. It also induces airflow, as do the windows, positioned

0 5 10

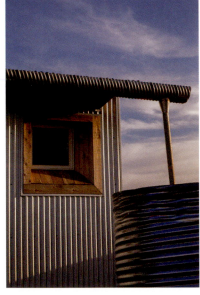

ABOVE The cabin sits on an open Texas plain with plenty of sunlight to fuel the photovoltaic solar panels, which power all the lights, kitchen appliances, and the electric composting toilet. Rainwater is collected for cleaning and bathing.

LEFT The rain barrel, gutter, and siding are all constructed of low-maintenance galvanized steel. The inset window reveals the thickness of the perimeter walls, which are stuffed with shredded-denim insulation.

Bath

Living

BLUE JEANS FOREVER

Denim insulation is made from 80-percent denim recycled from cast-off ripped and tattered jeans. It's a readily available product and has an energy-efficiency level slightly higher than fiberglass batt insulation. It is available in rolls or as loose fill, has no odor, is not itchy to install, and provides a great sound barrier. In the wrangler world of Texas, denim insulation was the perfect fit for this project.

ABOVE The cabin has no well; the "running" water supplying the kitchen and bathroom sinks (used for cleaning only, not drinking) and the shower (it's tucked in to the left of the towel rack) is gravity-fed unheated rainwater. The composting toilet is operated by electricity.

RIGHT Though modest, the kitchen contains an under-counter refrigerator, microwave, and an electric hotplate, adequate for a weekend's stay.

fore and aft on the narrow form. The soaring roof created the opportunity for a modest sleeping loft above the front porch.

The wood-framed walls and roof were built extra thick and stuffed with shredded-denim insulation (see the sidebar at left) to help moderate the temperature swings of the hot days and cool nights of West Texas. At less than 400 sq. ft., the cabin takes its cues from the Spartan use of space of Thoreau's Walden. A woodstove warms the interior on clear-sky winter nights. Professor Flueckiger noted that it was difficult to find a sufficiently small stove that wouldn't overheat this tiny space that's as well insulated as a thermos bottle.

When all was assembled, the cabin was transported 200 miles to land owned by the Pease River Foundation. With their mission of environmental quality, protection and beautification of natural resources, and wetlands conservation and management, they

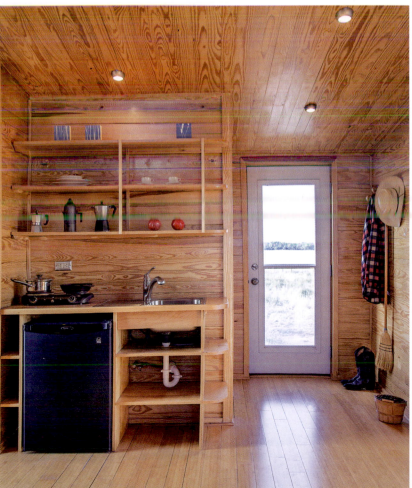

now have a demonstration sustainable residence that derives its electricity from the sun, harvests water from rainfall, and has a composting toilet. The cabin is utilized by a variety of short-term residents, from poets to scientists. Professor Flueckiger has enjoyed a few stays as well. Future classes will monitor the cabin's performance.

The well-insulated cabin needs only a tiny woodstove to keep it toasty warm, even when the wind is whipping across the plain. The walls are southern yellow pine, the floor is bamboo. The walls contain inset panels painted by Carol Flueckiger, Professor Flueckiger's wife, with quotes and signatures from Thoreau (right) and LeCorbusier.

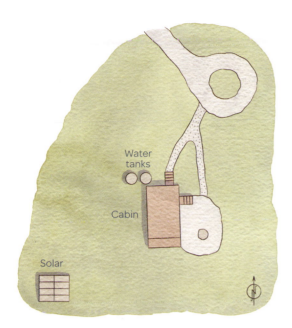

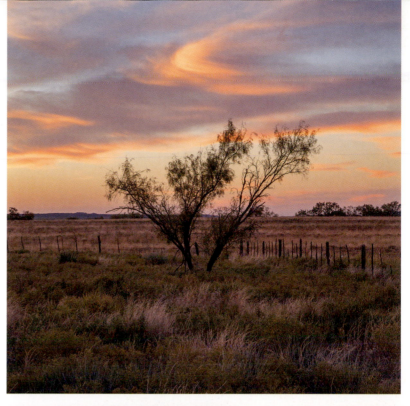

RIGHT A snug loft over the porch is large enough to accommodate several sleepers. The hatch in the ceiling is fitted with an acrylic ventilator that can pull the hot Texas air out of the cabin in summer.

BELOW Thin veneers of Baltic birch plywood were laminated and formed by students to create the stairs to the loft.

The living room and tower room face south, open to the sun's warming rays. The wood shingles on the cabin and the vertical wood siding on the tower are stained black, in keeping with the color of pine bark. The chimney stone is taconite from a nearby mine.

> "One of the assets of using recycled wood is that it comes with a story line, a pedigree."

THINKING LOCALLY

Empty-nester years were approaching when a Minnesota woman decided to recapture idyllic childhood memories of summers at the lake. With husband in tow, she looked for just the right property to build a cabin, finally deciding upon a lot with towering red pines set along the rocky shoreline of a northern Minnesota lake where I have my own cabin and have designed several others. I was brought in to design an enclave of structures for the couple, including a main cabin, garage/bunkroom, sauna, and guest cabin. Although the guest cabin has yet to be built, a boathouse was later added to the ensemble.

The main cabin is banked into a hill, facing the lake, with entry from the driveway at the middle level into a lofty mezzanine that overlooks the living space below. This floor also includes a bedroom and bath. The primary living areas (living/dining room area, kitchen, and the couple's bedroom) are on the ground floor, which opens out onto a porch and offers quick access to the lake and sauna. One level above the mezzanine is a perch, a tower view for vistas beyond their quiet bay out to the 23-mile-long lake.

Tower room

First floor

Second floor

TOP Located in the coldest region of Minnesota, the structure is banked into a hill on the north and east sides.

ABOVE The eastern entry, its extra-wide door painted a vibrant blueberry, is on the second level.

RIGHT The entry opens onto the second level adjacent to the loft. The kitchen tucks under the loft, its cabinets stained sumac red. The dining table and benches were made from a red pine tree taken from the site.

BELOW South- and west-facing cottage-style windows flood light into the living room. The fireplace is taconite, the wall paneling local aspen, and the beams recycled pine. The floor is linoleum, made in part from flax chaff.

Interest in using local materials led to an old friend of the couple, David Hozza, who was, at the time, dismantling a mammoth 1880s grain elevator in Superior, Wisconsin. The grain bins were constructed of old-growth white pine and years of use had worn them down to a silky, smooth patina. The bins were repurposed for use as structural timbers and paneling in the main cabin. The white pine was married with locally cut aspen (also used for paneling) and area-mined taconite stone (used in the construction of the fireplace) for a cabin that is a true reflection of the local natural resources.

Products that couldn't be sourced locally were considered for their "green" contribution. The flooring, for example, is linoleum, a by-product of flax production. And a tree that was felled to make room on the site for the cabin was milled and used to make the cabin's dining table and a set of benches.

WOOD WITH A PEDIGREE

If you are looking to add rustic character to your cabin, consider using recycled lumber. The reuse of building materials is as old as mankind. Recycled stone from ancient Rome can be found in buildings stretching from medieval times through modern day. In America, we often reuse materials taken from old warehouses, barns, and trestle bridges.

Saving worthy building materials from landfills and fire pits is a noble act, even if it is at times costly. But using recycled materials generally reduces the carbon footprint of a new building, particularly if the materials are found locally.

Old wood is stable and unlikely to crack and splinter further. It is, however, untested lumber (its structural capacity unknown) and may need to be oversized when used in bearing situations for safety's sake. All recycled lumber should be fumigated before reuse to eliminate the possibility of any insect infestation.

One of the assets of recycled wood is that it comes with a story line, a pedigree. It becomes part of the charming lore of your cabin tale, retold and embellished over decades and across generations.

TOP The second-floor bath has a fir door, linoleum floor, green glass and tile, and a fir ceiling recycled from an Illinois grain elevator.

LEFT The second-floor bedroom is partially in the tower and large enough for two beds. The storage door was crafted from recycled wood.

RIGHT Atop the tower is a multipurpose room that can be used for sleeping, reading, or gazing across the lake.

BELOW One of the three outbuildings is a wood-fired sauna. A fourth, a guest cabin, is planned for the rock ledge above the sauna.

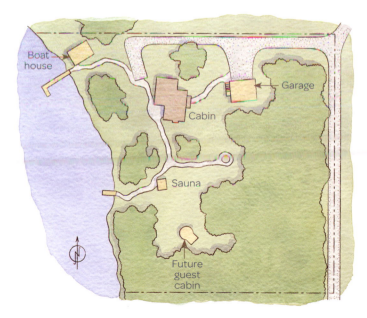

Boat house

Garage

Cabin

Sauna

Future guest cabin

The wooden tree-house cabin sits atop a stone-built lower level. The deck looks like a dock floating out into the treetops.

"A special place to relax, grounded in nature while suspended in the sky."

OPPOSITES ATTRACT

It is rare to find a two-story retreat where the levels have vastly contrasting characters. The Stoneflower cabin melds a cave-like grotto with a light-filled wooden tree house. Added to the experience is a dock-like deck that perches its users high in the treetops.

In the early 1960s, landscape architects Bob Shaheen and Curt Goodfellow were hired to aid in the development of Eden Isle, a residential community in central Arkansas. A portion of their fee was paid in the form of a challenging lot on which they decided to build a shared cabin. Familiarity led them to architect Fay Jones, and he to his favorite themes, the cave and the tree house. Jones was steeped in the organic architectural principles of his friend Frank Lloyd Wright, and he sought to blend the cabin into the land.

The cabin is approached through a walk in the forest and a gradual descent down a stony path. Entry is into an organically shaped stone-lined grotto. Its principal space is a sitting area fitted with stone ledge seats and a stone fireplace. Adjacent is a tight storage corridor that leads into a bathing area lit by a skylight. The bathroom features a stone ledge sink, and the shower cascades off rocks as if one were standing beneath a waterfall.

The deck is a special place to enjoy dining in a leafy environment. The structural cross bracing provides the cabin with a decorative crown.

FAR LEFT A circular stair connects the three levels of Stoneflower.

LEFT The dining space has a view back toward the entry.

BELOW The sleeping loft is tucked below the rafters, with a stunning view out over the living room to the deck outside.

From the grotto, a circular stair rises to the tree house. Here, a lofty narrow structure, 12 ft. wide, 30 ft. long, and 24 ft. tall, is filled with light from opposite ends. The kitchen, dining, and sitting areas share this space; overhead is a sleeping loft. The lattice-like structural framing that crowns the space secures the wind loads of the walls and supports the roof with its sizable overhangs.

Extending from the living space is a slender, 30-ft.-long deck, shaped like a boat dock jutting out into the treetops beyond. It is anchored on metal scaffolding piers, with the final section of deck a cantilever.

The cabin was completed in 1965, built for $25,000 and some landscaping sweat equity. In the warm summer climate of Arkansas, it features passive cooling, cool air rising from the forest floor, through the grotto, and up and out the windows just under the roof of the tree house. These windows are opened and closed through ropes and pulleys accessible from the tree-house floor.

The brilliance of Stoneflower was heralded in *Life* magazine in 1966 and was the prelude to Fay Jones's most renowned structure, Thorncrown Chapel. Although the property has passed through several owners, Stoneflower has been well stewarded, undoubtedly due to its owners' respect for it as a special place to relax, grounded in nature while suspended in the sky.

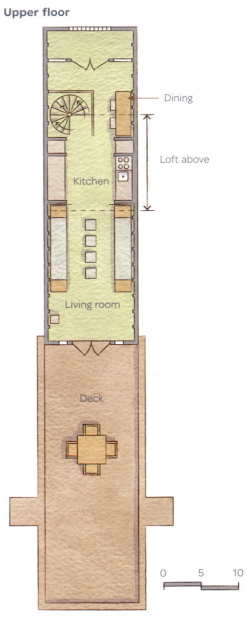

Upper floor

Dining

Loft above

Kitchen

Living room

Deck

0   5   10

Upper floor

TOP This cord is used to open the window ventilators high above the space.

ABOVE The stairs cascade down among the rocks toward the entry on the lower level.

The living room opens to the deck. Sliding doors can close the living room from the kitchen and dining area.

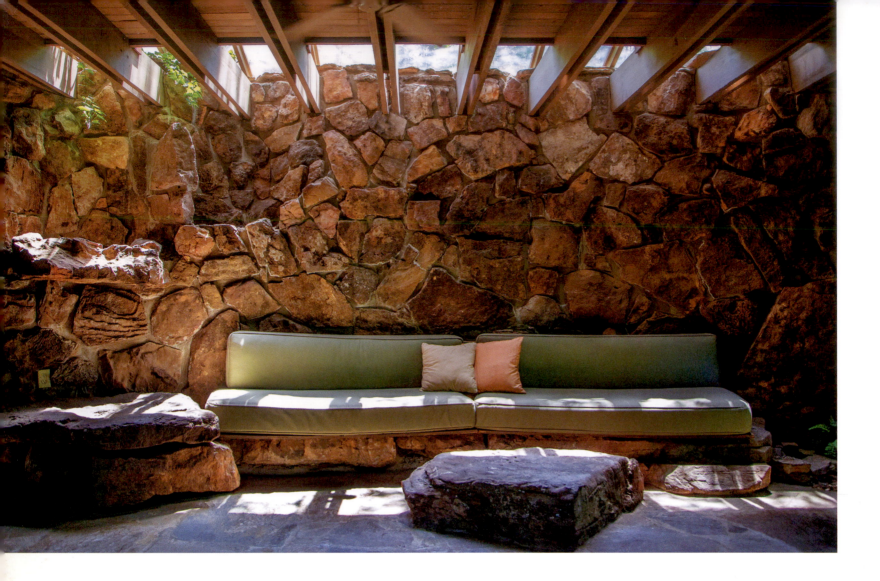

CUTAWAY VIEW

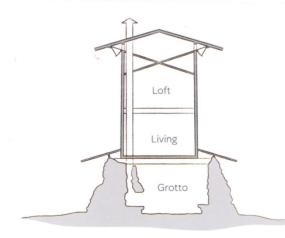

An architect's design for a cabin can often be recognized as unique from others because of its rigorous study of the structure in cross section. Floor plans are prepared in the construction of all buildings, but it is the cross section that aids in the full exploitation of interior space.

The lower organic level of Stoneflower can easily be understood by examining the floor plan. The tree house, however, is a brilliant exploration of cross section and the transformation of standard framing lumber into a lacy tree-like canopy.

Lower floor

Entry

Bathing

Pool

Living area

Fireplace

Terrace

0   5   10

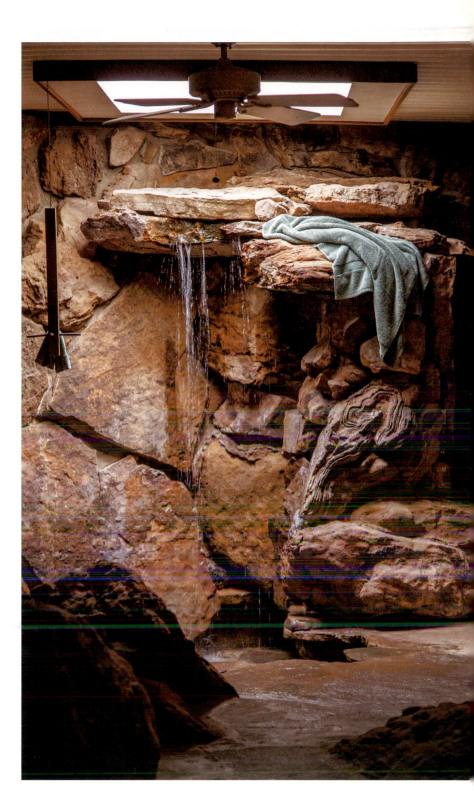

RIGHT The lower grotto features a shower that appears to cascade down from the rocks. The water controls are hidden around the corner.

OPPOSITE The lower-level grotto provides a cool escape from the heat of Arkansas summer days. The space is illuminated with natural light from the windows above.

Cabin design and construction are an opportunity to express the spirit of the place, a client's unique interests, and the whimsy **JUST FOR THE FUN OF IT** of architects and builders. Cabins are made particular and often fanciful through family lore, family artifacts, and the work of generations of amateur artists and craftsmen who dare to try something different.

"Would the concrete floors of Sri Lanka be appropriate?"

BASE CAMP FOR FUN

Pixie Martin first arrived at Madeline Island in Wisconsin in the early 1980s as a coed in search of a summer job. For many summers since, the island has been a place for Pixie to hang out, filled with friends and days spent bicycling, kayaking, sailing, and swimming. Now, with her husband, Jay Estling, and son, Micah, she has her own base camp for fun, a modest cabin in the woods.

Through their work, Jay and Pixie have traveled the globe, from Third World backwaters to Geneva, Switzerland. For many years they'd kept a home in Minneapolis, but their annual summer sojourns to Madeline Island made them question where home base should be. Realizing that a cabin of their own on the island would let them come and go at will (and give them a place to store their summer toys), they sold their Minneapolis home and bought a 5 acre wooded lot on the island.

I first spoke to Pixie and Jay when they called me from Geneva. I'd just completed a larger structure on the island, but the couple knew from my earlier book *The Cabin* that I'd be comfortable designing something smaller...and something fun.

LEFT The cabin opens up on the south side to a screened porch and French doors accessing the patio.

OPPOSITE Porch living was an important consideration in the design of this cabin. An overhead fan provides a breeze when nature does not.

ABOVE A garage with guest lodging above greets visitors to this island cabin. Similarly clad in red roof and bark-colored siding, the two buildings form an ensemble in the forest.

RIGHT The living room is compact and cozy but made to feel larger with French doors that open to the outside. You can see the framing of the second floor, with its fir beams and pine decking. A view, woodstove, and television compete for attention in the living room.

First floor

Bedroom

Entry

Living

Dining

Kitchen

Screened porch

Terrace

0   5   10

A desk and corner reading/sleeping alcove are located at the back of the living/dining room area. The material palette for the space includes birch walls, fir beams and trim, and a bronze-stained concrete floor.

ISLAND TIME

Time on islands has its own pace and often ebbs and flows with the rhythm of the ferry schedule. Small, low-populated islands have few services focused on building, but lots catering to seasonal tourism. On Madeline Island it is easy to buy a T-shirt or embossed fishing cap, but don't bother looking for a 2×4 or a bag of nails.

All materials and often the laborers to assemble them have the added cost of ferry tariffs and ferry time. Even the concrete mixer truck rumbles onto the ferry.

And on small islands everyone knows everybody else's business. Whose brother did you not use as your electrician? Why did I see Bob on the golf course today when he hasn't finished my landscaping? I heard you paid a gold mine for those light fixtures!

A 20-minute ferry ride is the first taste of relaxation for Madeline Island residents.

Pixie and Jay's travels had made them aware of many forms of architecture and they had a great appreciation for a wide variety of materials. Would the concrete floors of Sri Lanka be appropriate? How about the arches of the Middle East? They sought an architectural approach that was appropriate to the land and region. The couple knew that a traditional approach on the outside would show respect for the neighbors, but a modern glassy interior would bring the beauty of the outside into the interior. As architects, we are taught to edit, and thus the concrete floors were in, the arches out, and a vernacular form with lots of cottage-style windows seemed just the ticket.

ABOVE An outdoor shower is always exhilarating after a rigorous island bicycle ride. As a backdrop, the textures and colors used on the exterior of the cabin are all drawn from the surrounding landscape.

LEFT The kitchen is conveniently located to serve the dining area and porch.

Second floor

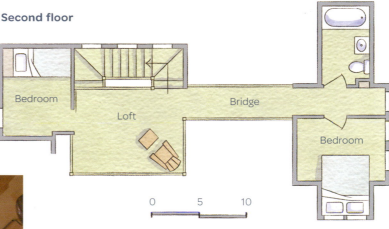

Bedroom

Loft

Bridge

Bedroom

0   5   10

The loft provides additional space to sit and relax. Down the "bridge" hallway are a bedroom and bathroom.

Jay felt that a cabin was incomplete without a screened porch, and Pixie wanted a terrace in the sun. They both knew that bigger wasn't better and preferred small inviting spaces to grand and palatial. Thus the cabin has a porch and a terrace, three cozy bedrooms, and a living room and loft with niches. Local materials of yellow birch and pine were mixed in with the structural fir.

The forested site was flat and low, with some wetlands areas that were unbuildable. To limit excavation, we opted for flat slab construction; we protected the trees on site as best we could and Pixie and Jay seeded the disturbed area in wildflowers. (Neither Pixie nor Jay saw themselves taking time out from relaxation to mow the grass.) The few trees that were removed were cut into slabs, dried, and fashioned into a dining room table and bench.

The porch overlooks the lake with both screened and unscreened sections. The tail ends of ridge logs decorate the gable end of the cabin.

"Where better place to tell a tall fishing tale than in a century-old log lodge?"

WE TOOK TO THE WOODS

Fishing camps are part of the rich legacy of Maine's north woods, where wild brook trout, lake trout, and inland salmon are prized catches, whatever your method of hooking them might be. Not surprisingly, this area has an abundance of fishing camps, some of which date back to the 1800s, when trains made traveling to the region more feasible for the urban populations of Portland, Portsmouth, Boston, and beyond.

The older camps are revered for their history, lore, and nostalgia. Where better place to tell a tall fishing tale than in a century-old log lodge? New additions are planned with great care so as to blend in with the spirit of the old camp.

Architect Sam Van Dam of Portland, Maine, was asked to add a new residence to a classic fishing camp deep in the Maine back country. The owner wanted to include a bathroom and a modest kitchen, along with sitting areas both inside and out. He also asked that the structure be able to sleep up to eight fishermen. Because of the cabin's location deep in the woods, the client wanted a soaring interior space that was open to light, in contrast to the small dark spaces usually found in older camps in the region.

OPPOSITE Sam Van Dam's sketches for this cabin are worthy of framing.

ABOVE The stair to the sleeping lofts rises behind the fireplace.

LEFT AND OPPOSITE A cathedral-like space awaits cabin goers in the living room. The tree trunks were handpicked for their vertical lines. Local stones were used to build the fireplace.

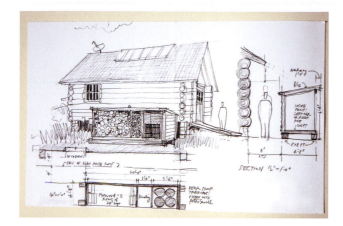

Van Dam designed a 20-ft.-tall living room with a loft overlook above. Two bedroom wings flank the central space on the main floor and two bunk alcoves were created in the loft. The natural taper of the cedar columns creates a Gothic cathedral–like experience. The fireplace, built from local split stone, rises high into the space. Van Dam decided to use Western red cedar logs, known for their durability, for the addition. The logs were cut, notched, and assembled in British Columbia, and then numbered, dismantled, and shipped to Maine for reassembly.

Van Dam describes the design as a "throwback to an earlier era, completely one with its surroundings." To sit on the porch, gazing across the meadow while tying a fly, is a timeless experience in any century.

First floor

ABOVE The Western red cedar beam and post are beautifully joined at the porch. Local artist John Bryan carved the god of wind, Aeolus, flushing up some fowl, into the end of the beam.

RIGHT The porch was designed to give floor-to-ceiling views to the lake.

Cabin

LOG SHRINKAGE

When trees are cut and moisture begins to evaporate, the trunks shrink in diameter but not in length. Log-house designs often call for the logs to be laid horizontally in perimeter walls and vertically as interior or porch roof supports. In such cases, the differential settlement between the shrinkage in the walls and no shrinkage of the columns requires the installation of column jacks. In the early years of the structure, the columns can be jacked down as needed to maintain a level roof. After a decade, the settlement is relatively complete and the jacks can be removed.

Loft

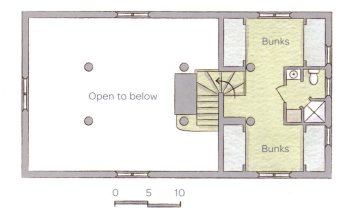

Bunks

Open to below

Bunks

0 5 10

ABOVE The loft bed is nestled in under the roof. A window opens up the snug space and allows for welcome breezes and morning light.

LEFT An antique desk awaits letter writers and map readers seeking that special fishing hole.

A water tower was added to the cabin during its early days to provide a
reliable source of water for priming the well pump.

"Walter took the unusual step of adding a water tower atop the kitchen."

A WORK IN PROGRESS

Walter Johnson started building the family cabin in his teens, about the time he began architecture school at the University of Minnesota in 1917. His parents, Carl and Hilma Johnson, had purchased three 50-ft. lots on Battle Lake not far from their home in Fargo, North Dakota. Carl sited the first structure, a simple rectangular cabin, and left young Walter and his mother in charge of building it. In short order they completed the two-bedroom cabin, and summers at the lake fast became a family tradition.

The untimely death of his father interrupted Walter's architectural studies, and it wasn't long before he took over the family construction business in Fargo. Marriage and two children were soon to follow—as was the need to add on to the cabin to accommodate the necessities of summer living.

An appended summer kitchen was the first addition (to reduce heat buildup in the cabin), followed by a third bedroom and a screened porch. By the 1930s, the family decided to add more living space facing the lake.

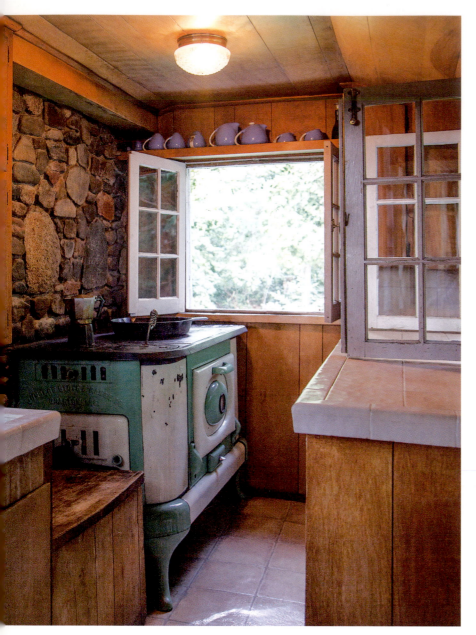

The Depression years were trying ones for Walter's business and he accepted modest remodeling projects as a way to make ends meet. Discarded doors, windows, and lumber from these projects found their way into the cabin, and their variation in size and shape added an eclectic charm.

Walter's mother, Hilma, had emigrated from Sweden, where a proper structure was always skirted in stone to protect it from grass fires, preserve the wood framing, and keep out varmints. Walter scoured the area farm fields for discarded rock piles and amassed enough for a stone base and, later, two fireplaces.

Hand-dug wells of the day were none too reliable and needed water for priming, so Walter took the unusual step of adding a water tower atop the kitchen. The graceful tower adds a fitting crown to the ensemble of shapes that now comprises the cabin.

ABOVE This old summer kitchen was built onto the side of the house to get the heat of cooking out of the center of the cabin.

RIGHT The cabin was built just steps away from Battle Lake.

SECOND TIME'S THE CHARM

The recycling of building materials into cabin construction has a rich tradition. The casual nature of cabin architecture, the do-it-yourself construction ethic, and pay-as-you-go cabin financing all play a role in this pattern of reuse. Floorboards from high school gyms, windows from churches, portholes from boats, and grandma's discarded kitchen cabinets can all find their way into one owner's cabin.

You can find these materials at recycling centers, architectural antique stores, and salvage yards, and then there is good old dumpster diving. Using secondhand materials may require adding time for refurbishing and installation, but they also add to the lore of one's own cabin.

ABOVE The cabin was built in many phases, often with salvaged house parts, such as the windows in the living room.

BELOW One of the latest additions was the living room, with its fieldstone fireplace. The chimney was built from stones rolled smooth by glaciers, collected from nearby fields.

LEFT A bright, cheery morning space greets breakfast folks with a fresh breeze and the smell of the forest.

BELOW The bunkroom was made to be narrow like a ship's berth. Each bunk gets its own window.

OPPOSITE The Johnson cabin has seen many additions over many years, yet the whole ensemble makes for a charming composition.

Living room

Bunk room

Bedroom

Bedroom

Bedroom

Dining room

Entry

Bedroom

Kitchen

Deck

Porch room

Summer kitchen

0   5   10

As grandchildren arrived, more sleeping space was necessary. A bunkroom was constructed in a lean-to off the living room, and the three existing bedrooms were enlarged and enhanced with corner windows. Walter's work seemed never done, but he always preferred tinkering with the cabin to fishing or taking things easy. He added window seats, vaulted ceilings, and charming embellishments until he was disabled by a stroke in 1973.

The cabin has since been inherited by his two sons, who have four children of their own. Generations now scattered across the United States return home to Walter's creation on the shore of Battle Lake. Daughter-in-law Harriet Johnson noted, "Like most Minnesota family cabins that have survived five generations, it holds an atmosphere of many stories, a jumble of furniture styles, and an attitude of, what shall we invent to solve this crazy problem?"

> "They trekked through a stand of pines, then up and over a rocky rise to look out over the frozen lake below."

ELFIN HEAVEN

Herb Pilhofer and his wife, Rosemary Januschka, had for many years enjoyed journeying from St. Paul to their log cabin in western Wisconsin. But their babies soon grew up into active children who attended weekend soccer tournaments and music recitals. Opportunities for weekends at the cabin became so infrequent that the couple reluctantly decided to sell their retreat.

Fast forward 10 years and Herb and Rosemary were newly minted empty nesters, with a renewed yearning for solitude and fresh air. But this time they wanted to push even deeper into the Wisconsin woods, with a cabin set on a spring-fed lake, surrounded by stands of pine and birch.

Searching online, Rosemary found a promising property but had a difficult time finding a realtor who would lace up snow-shoes and take them to see it. She and Herb had already decided that they would both have to swoon before agreeing to a purchase. And swoon they did as they trekked through a stand of pines, then up and over a rocky rise to look out over the frozen lake below. The acreage was large enough to ensure privacy and a serene solitude.

LEFT Cottage-style windows, with a smaller upper sash and a larger lower, are used on three sides of this glassy lake-view porch. The floor is slate.

OPPOSITE The structural tree columns used in the construction of this cabin make visitors feel as if they have stumbled upon a magical elfin wonderland in the forest.

203

Main floor

Herb and Rosemary sought a design that would stand in contrast to the heavy, dark log cabin they had previously owned. They described to Deane Hillbrand, a timber framer and design enthusiast, a hobbit-like house, built with a sense of whimsy and fun. Herb's European background suggested an alpine motif, making use of stucco and timber accents.

Herb noted that he had to cajole and coax the craftsmen on the job to join in the improvisational nature of the project, but once they did, the straight lines of traditional timber framing gave way to curves, windows danced into playful locations, and stone cascaded down, seemingly rooting the cabin into the surrounding landscape.

Hillbrand contributed his signature black ash timbers, inside and out, cut from the grove behind his own log home in Minnesota. He furnished and cut the recycled fir timbers that give the ceiling its backbone. Carpenter Nick Allen fabricated all the built-ins—window seats, staircase, cabinets, and closet doors—using cherry wood with bark edges for some of them. He added trim and interior detail everywhere. After Herb and Rosemary bought a dining table, Nick fashioned built-in benches for it.

Nick's colleague Dave Tworek executed Deane's idea of using glass blocks for the ceiling in the first-floor bathroom, as well as placing two recycled stained-glass windows in the lower hallway. He also built the sauna and the structure housing the hot tub. Mason Tony Van Selius worked with stone he culled onsite, with the help of Herb's tractor. With his stone stash, Tony built support posts, a fireplace, and a retaining wall.

Now Herb and Rosemary retreat to their "hobbit" house with glee. They round the bend of the driveway to see the roll of the eyebrow wall over the garage, the wisp of the curved stucco forms, and the forest of trees encompassing the porch. They often step outside to listen to the breeze in the pines, the tinkle of bell chimes hidden in the trees, and the lapping of waves.

Lower floor

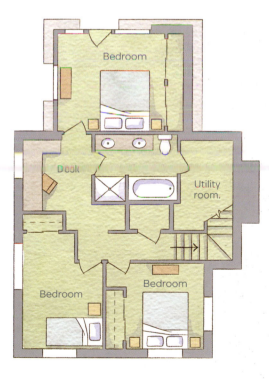

ABOVE The glass blocks set into the floor to the right of the stairs drop light into the bathroom below. The stair rail, crafted from cherry wood, has a lyrical quality, like notes on a scale.

OPPOSITE The stone fireplace separates the living room from the entry and stairwell. Its design was left to the creative energy of mason Tony Van Selius; the stone used to construct it was collected from the property.

LEFT Built-in sofas set into each window of the living room are long and wide enough to accommodate an overflow of overnight guests.

ABOVE A picnic shelter 50 yd. from the cabin allows for alfresco dining lakeside.

Upper floor

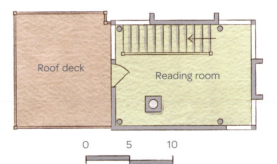

Roof deck

Reading room

0   5   10

The majestic pines are a delightfully scented setting for the hot tub experience. It sits atop a rock ledge with a view to the lake.

FINDING THE PERFECT SPOT

Finding the ideal property takes patience and some tenacity. Establishing goals for the search—budget, desired character of the landscape, distance from the primary home—will help the buyer and any realtors commissioned to aid in the search. The attributes of the site trump those of any buildings, as structures can be remodeled or replaced, budget permitting.

The Pilhofers have owned three vacation properties and have some suggestions for the search:

• Familiarize yourself with the area you are interested in. Drive through it not once but several times. Don't be timid about talking with locals. Ask about the water quality of the lakes and streams, any mining operations nearby, and access to services like hospitals, supermarkets, and boat service.

• Consider availing yourself of local realtors; they're more likely to know of long-term owners ready to sell.

• One-stop shopping can be achieved by attending sportsmen shows that feature realtors.

• Don't trust a realtor's picture-taking skills. You must see the property to experience the "This is it!" moment.

Picnic shelter

Garage

Hot tub

Cabin

The cabin and garage are positioned to form a protected courtyard
out of the wind.

> "A detached garage with
> a sleeping garret above
> provides a perfect getaway
> for rambunctious teenagers."

BOARDING HOUSE

When it comes to time at the cabin, fun can take many forms. For the Baker family it is all about outdoor recreation with family and friends. Bruce and Kathy purchased a lot in the Giants Ridge Recreational Development in Minnesota, three hours away from their city home, because they knew the development's focus on skiing, golfing, and hiking and biking trails, plus its location on a series of connected lakes, would provide ample opportunity for fresh-air fun.

The Bakers purchased a flat lot atop a plateau with a majestic view to Wynne Lake and the ski hill beyond. I was brought in, along with my colleague Chris Meyer, to design a modest cabin (though they wanted it to be able to sleep 10) that would be easy to use and maintain and possess sufficient storage space for the family's considerable recreational equipment.

In the design we developed, the axis of the dining space captures the picture-postcard lake view at one end and serves as the portal to an outdoor terrace. The main gabled living space opens to the south, capturing welcome light and warmth during the colder months. A large loft floats above the social space and provides overflow sleeping when necessary, as well a stunning view of the Mesabi Iron Range. Two modest bedrooms and baths are tucked into the northeast end of the cabin, along with the furnace room, laundry, and stairs. A glassed-in porch serves both as entry and a

LEFT Cabins are also about enjoying the out of doors, and the Bakers love to sit by their campfire.

LEFT BOTTOM The dining table is positioned so that everyone at the table can enjoy the bucolic view of the lake. The dining room itself extends to an outdoor terrace.

OPPOSITE TOP Light and view dominate the living and dining areas of the cabin, while an open loft floats above, supported on fir beams.

OPPOSITE BOTTOM The enclosed porch is located away from the view on the sunny side of the cabin. Quad-hung storm windows can be opened wide on hot summer days to catch the breezes; closed, they hold in the heat and extend the use of the porch into spring and fall.

First floor

Terrace

Dining

Bedroom

Living

Kitchen

Laundry

Screened porch

0   5   10

relaxing spot to catch the morning sun and avoid cold winds out of the northwest.

A detached garage with a sleeping garret above provides storage, project space, and a perfect getaway for rambunctious teenagers. As more adult toys and a new motorcycle have arrived, another storage shed is being contemplated for future construction.

The cabin walls are constructed of vertical insulated concrete forms, which provide more than enough insulation in one of the coldest regions in the lower 48. A radiant-heat poured concrete floor is easy to maintain and provides even heat distribution. A Danish woodstove can take away whatever chill remains in the air and warm frosty toes after a long day on the boards.

BETTER INSULATION THROUGH CONCRETE

Insulated concrete forms (ICFs) are comprised of two outer walls of rigid Styrofoam® with a voided cavity between, which is then filled with concrete. The form is held together with neoprene flanges to prevent blowout of the concrete as it dries and sets up. The flanges, located every 8 in. to 16 in. along the blocks, are arranged to carry either vertical or horizontal reinforcing bars, which are needed to increase concrete strength.

The dimensions of the foam walls and concrete core can vary, depending upon insulation needs, the structural strength desired, and the unique method used by each manufacturer to create their product. High-energy-performance walls are easily achieved because of the lack of energy transfer in the Styrofoam, the inability of wind to penetrate the wall, and the storage of heat in the concrete. Cabins built using ICF forms have high wind-shear properties and are touted for the quietness of the space enclosed.

ABOVE The surrounding forest provides plenty of wood to keep Sonny warm. It also helps that there is radiant heat in the concrete floor.

LEFT Working in the kitchen is made more pleasurable by the spectacular view out the windows. The cabinets are stock items purchased from a big box store.

Second floor

Loft

Bedroom

0 5 10

LEFT Depending on the season, various types of recreational equipment can be found around the cabin.

BELOW Because it is open on three sides, with windows all around, the loft bedroom feels as though it is floating over the space below. Metal railings add to the open feeling.

Porch cabins and glassy retreats have been around for centuries but are now being reinterpreted in climates across North

LIGHT AND AIR America, including four-season structures. Sites are selected for their natural beauty, and architects are making use of technological advances to design cabins with a new-found openness that are warm, secure, and in aesthetic harmony with their surroundings.

The cabin is perched on a knoll with views of the Berkshire Mountains beyond. The openness of this cabin connects it to a larger landscape.

> "The doors to the porch are flung open and the whole interior of the cabin feels as if it is outside."

ONE BIG ROOM

"Nothing can beat a great hike followed by a great dinner and great music," notes Todd, explaining why he and his wife, Martha, have been coming to the Berkshires in Massachusetts from Boston for nearly 20 years. It's music that first drew them to the area; Martha performs here every year as a member of the Tanglewood Festival Chorus.

In November 2005 Todd and Martha were out for a drive in the area when they took a random turn down a random road and saw a "land for sale" sign. On a lark they drove in and immediately loved the site, a rolling, forested hillside. There were views to the mountains in the distance as well as to a small lake across the road. "We decided that starting with the perfect spot was more important than the house, so we took the plunge," says Todd.

Four years later they engaged Boston architect MaryAnn Thompson to design a retreat cabin. They wanted a structure that would be rustic and cozy, yet offer modern amenities. They were enamored of the idea of a single great room for cooking, eating, socializing, and sleeping. With two children, Todd and Martha felt their cabin experience should be more about bonding and less about privacy.

ABOVE This cabin is about one-room living; the kitchen and living room open into each other, with bed alcoves at the end of the space. Togetherness and bonding are preferred by the family over privacy.

LEFT The window grids have a lyrical quality, appropriate for this cabin with musical roots.

OPPOSITE The two sleeping spaces, one with bunk beds, have a divider in between and a curtain for visual privacy from the living room. Windows in each sleeping space connect sleepers with morning light.

The site had a natural clearing, but they decided instead to nestle the cabin up to the forest's edge. MaryAnn designed the cabin so that the angle of the roof parallels the slope of the hill. East-facing windows look out to the clearing and the west wall is banked into the hill with high clerestory windows.

The structure is modular post and beam, with six structural bays. The middle two bays encompass the kitchen and dining and living areas; the south two bays comprise a screened-in porch. The northern two bays are two sleeping alcoves with a sleeping loft above. The floors were built with radiant heating.

Todd and Martha utilize their cabin year round. During the summer, the doors to the porch are flung open and the whole interior of the cabin feels as if it is outside. In the winter they can remotely activate the cabin's radiant heating before leaving Boston. The cabin is just 15 minutes away from a ski slope, which they have a view of once the leaves come down.

Todd and Martha intend to develop the cabin into a full-time home, but for the time being the joys of sharing the big-room cabin are putting no rush on future construction.

A compact bathroom is made to feel more spacious with a high ceiling and light from above. The walls surrounding the tub are finished in a charcoal-hued slate, providing a complementary contrast to the red cedar paneling used for the other walls.

ABOVE This sleeping loft is a new take on the porch bed. The built-in beds above the screened-in porch allow sleepers to enjoy the coolness of night-time breezes.

ABOVE RIGHT The sleeping loft presents an overlook to the porch. The floor is stained and scored concrete.

Bedroom

Living room

Porch

Bed-room

Storage

0   5   10

STEWARDS OF THE FOREST

This cabin was one of the first structures designed to comply with the Berkshire Scenic Mountain Act. Adopted in 2006, this program requires that a house not lift above the tree line, that tree cutting be limited to a quarter acre, and that drainage be designed to prevent both flooding and erosion of the site. Its purpose is to protect the scenic highlands and slopes along with the water resources the family comes here to enjoy.

RIGHT The birch cabinets, windows, fir beams, and red cedar paneling create a contemporary composition of linear lines in contrast to the organic lines of nature beyond.

The bay of windows offers an arcing view to the lake beyond. The stained concrete floor is equipped with radiant heat, while additional heat and ambience are provided by a European woodstove fueled by deadfall trees from the property.

"A modern cabin, cozy in the winter, yet airy and open to summer breezes."

PANORAMIC VIEW

One of the biggest challenges an architect faces when designing a lakeside cabin is making the most of the views. In a perfect world, the lake will be visible from every room, allowing guests and owners to have plenty of opportunities to catch a glimpse of the loons, see which lakeside neighbor is skimming by in their canoe, or enjoy the tranquility of the moon's reflection as it comes off the lake's surface at twilight.

Joe and Kris Plank had selected a retreat site in northeastern Minnesota seven hours from their home in Iowa. They loved its diverse forest of pine and birch, its large boulders and glacial rock, but most of all they loved its view over the lake. They could imagine family and friends gathered around a campfire outside, savoring a meal of just-caught fish, and teaching grandchildren to snowshoe. They asked me to capture all of this in a design for a modern cabin, cozy in the winter yet airy and open to summer breezes.

The result was a cabin under the cover of a single broad gabled metal roof. The floor plan features a sweeping arc that offers a panoramic view. The first floor consists of the couple's bedroom and the living areas. A screened porch extends beyond the arc but is still under the big roof. The two second-floor bedrooms open onto a deck that projects beyond the roof. High in the ridge of the gable is a child's garret.

A single metal roof covers the cabin and porch. The curved prow provides the foundation for a roof deck to enjoy lake views and stargazing. A garage, built in a similar form, is situated uphill from the cabin.

TOP RIGHT The roof drops low to the east over the porch so as to minimize the view to the neighbor. Site-selected rocks were used to build a retaining wall along the path to the lake.

RIGHT The entry faces south, with the roof overhang offering protection from the rain and snow. The cabin is sided in cedar shingles except at the entry, where it is fir plywood.

At the back of the cabin, away from the view, are the kitchen, bathrooms, laundry, and stair. This interior "wet wall" is easier to keep warm in Minnesota's cold winters; it is also easier to drain the pipes when closing down the cabin because of their short runs. A small office, which provides an overflow sleeping area, looks over the entry. A small mechanical room for the furnace and well equipment is situated below the main floor under the couple's bedroom, accessible from a trap door in the winter and utility doors from the outside.

For a modern, heat-efficient twist, the Planks chose to have stained concrete floors with radiant heat. Their island countertop is also concrete. The site has been landscaped and finished with a garage and dock. But the crowning glory remains their stunning view, enjoyed from most any room in the cabin in any weather, any season, and any time of day or night.

First floor

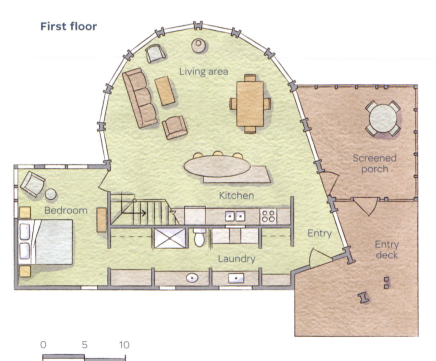

OPPOSITE TOP The kitchen is at the center of the cabin plan, convenient to the dining area and porch. The island, topped by concrete and wood, provides a nice contrast of color and material to the light wood cabinets.

OPPOSITE BOTTOM Built-in storage for sound equipment nestles under the stair, while exposed paralam ceiling beams and the pine decking of the second floor provide interest above. The door opens to the main-floor bedroom.

RIGHT These kayaks get great use in the adjoining lake, nearby Lake Superior, and the Boundary Waters Canoe Area Wilderness.

Second floor

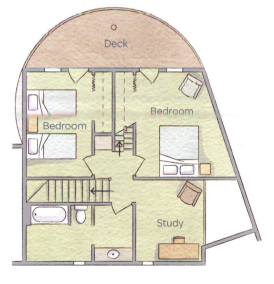

0   5   10

OPENING VIEWS WITH A GABLE FACE

No matter what style of house it is used with, a gable face can maximize views, making it a particularly good choice when designing a lakeside cabin. The principal roof loads are carried to ridge beams and side walls. Because of this, many cabin designs with gable faces feature prow forms to capture panoramic views. These often employ large expanses of glass both horizontally and vertically. However, because the view from the Plank cabin faces north into cold winds, the arc includes only a horizontal expanse, so as to minimize heat loss.

A cluster of four cabins is woven into the forest setting.

"Waking up in the glassed-in space makes you feel as if you are outside in the forest."

LIGHT SHEDS

The Gulf Islands, west of Vancouver, have been referred to as the Caribbean of the Northwest, providing a sunny respite from an otherwise cloudy region of Canada. A necklace of islands, they are surrounded by sheltered waters, strong tides, and dramatic coastlines. Lush with vegetation, the islands support considerable bird life. It's a magical retreat from the demands of urban living.

Architects Andrew Latreille and Mark Osburn of Osburn/Clarke Productions, Inc., were asked to design four separate sleeping cabins, each with two bedrooms, a bathroom, and an outdoor deck with views to the Strait of Georgia for a Portland, Oregon, family. The firm had already done work for the family, designing and building communal buildings that were part of this vacation compound.

The cabins are set along the shore but purposefully not in formation; rather, there is a higgledy-piggledy casualness employed. They are simple shed forms that open to the light, forest, and water through high glass walls that wrap around each side. Mark Osburn refers to them as "little sweetheart buildings,

ABOVE The building materials are elegantly limited to black metal, the golden patina of fir, and glass, used to open the interior space up to and frame the surrounding landscape.

OPPOSITE Each of the cabins opens to a spectacular view of Puget Sound.

Deck

Bedroom

Bunk-room

0   5   10

they speak for themselves." The interiors are clad in Douglas fir, the exteriors in Western red cedar, both native to the area.

The cabins are utilized only in the summer months; a woodstove is all the heating needed to take the chill off a cool evening. Photovoltaic solar panels located on the roofs store enough energy to supply the modest electrical demands. The buildings can be shut down for the winter season, with large sliding shutters and roll-downs over the windows and doors.

The sleeping sheds have been a big hit with family and friends, where waking up in the glassed-in space makes you feel as if you are outside in the forest. Whether relaxing on the deck with a good book or star-gazing at midnight, these special cabins make for a memorable getaway.

Metal roll-down shutters (you can see the bottom of the shutters just above the sliding glass doors) and wooden sliding barn doors can close up this structure to bad weather or secure it during the off-season.

Clerestory windows extend the view into the tree canopy to enhance the feeling of living outdoors.

PEN STROKES

Elegant, simple designs are often the result of a minimal sketch that presents an idea worthy of development. The challenge in development is to continue to edit the design while retaining its simplicity. Mark's initial elevation sketch for the Gulf Island cabins possessed all that was needed to direct this design into building.

A simple sketch of a few lines and a dab of color crystallizes the cabin concept.

Like a bridge into the forest, the cabin spans a dry creek bed. Its siting takes advantage of the natural shade and was carefully planned so as to minimize tree loss; only three needed to be removed.

"With room for 16, a whole Boy Scout troop can sleep over."

SCREEN PLAY

Austin, Texas, architect Henry Panton's client wanted his family and guests to experience fresh air in a country setting of 40 acres of pine forest located half an hour outside a small Texas town and adjacent to a state park. The design he came up with takes its inspiration from an historic form: the Texas bunkhouse, a barracks-like structure used to house working cowboys on western ranches (see "Bunk Up" on p. 240). Panton added a contemporary twist, a two-story 19-ft.-tall screened porch that runs the length of the house, opening up the interior to cool breezes and providing plenty of communal space for socializing and relaxing.

The bunkhouse is built across a dry creek bed. This lifts the structure off the ground, allowing air to flow freely under and around the porch, providing additional cooling. Only four trees needed to be removed to nestle the structure into the forest, which affords ample shade. Notes Panton, "It does get hot in Texas, however, the heavy shade of the pines provides a temperate climate with flora and wildlife."

LEFT Entry to the bunkhouse is through the screened porch. The exterior local cedar is stained variegated red around the whole of the bunkroom, including inside the porch.

BELOW These Texas-sized bunk beds were designed by Henry Panton. They are on casters so they can be easily rearranged or moved onto the porch for fresh-air sleeping. The many windows and overhead fans maximize ventilation and night-time breezes.

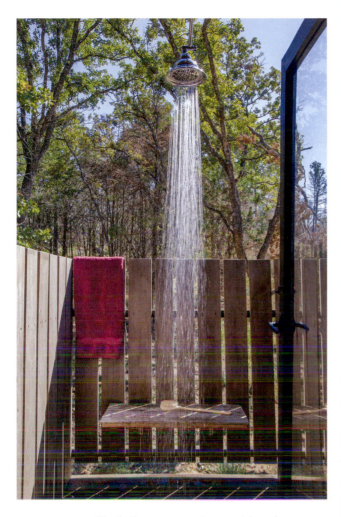

ABOVE The bathroom opens to an outdoor shower— the cabin's only shower.

RIGHT All dining and socializing occur in the 19-ft.-tall porch. Tigerwood is used on the floor and the table top, also designed by Panton.

The bunkroom contains four queen-size bunks designed by Panton for a Texas-size sleeping experience. With room for 16, a whole Boy Scout troop can sleep over. The grown-ups' bedroom is at the other end of the sleeping area, away from the hubbub of youthful sleepovers but close enough for supervision. In between are the kitchen and bathroom. An outdoor shower is cantilevered over the creek bed, making for a unique bathing experience.

BUNK UP

The bunkhouse, barracks, and dormitory share a common attribute of basic sheltered sleeping space: economy trumps privacy. Bunk beds are the preferred sleeping arrangement. Traditionally the cowboy bunkhouse had exterior toilets, usually outhouses, as well as an exterior bathing area and separate mess hall.

Bunkhouses are primitive in construction, using local materials and prevailing building methods. Occasionally they were heated with a woodstove but most were seasonal buildings.

Local zoning codes may allow a bunkhouse to be built as an auxiliary structure to a primary cabin or home. Some codes limit their size and/or mandate that they be without plumbing. The Texas bunkhouse has plumbing, heating, and air-conditioning for year-round comfort.

The mahogany screen door has muntins designed to evoke the spirit of the forest beyond. Metal rods give necessary lateral bracing to the tall but lightly framed porch.

A short distance from the bunkhouse is an organically designed pool and shade canopy. Local stone was used for the patio and low sitting walls situated beside the pool.

Shower

Bedroom

Kitchen

Screened porch

Bunk-room

0   5   10

The outside of the bunkhouse is sided with horizontal cedar boards stained barn red. The stain is washed into the boards to create a variegated tone that suggests age. The cedar extends into the porch to allude to its being an outside room. Metal is used on the roofing and railings, which are designed in a tree-branch motif. Metal French doors can be opened up to the porch for an almost outdoor sleeping experience.

Panton enjoys designing buildings "that are relevant to their surroundings with a strong sense of place." His sky-rise porch in the towering loblolly pines of this rural site is proof of his intent.

The porch sits atop a knoll overlooking a pond near the entry to the property. It is well protected from the hot Carolina sun under a canopy of trees.

"High in the porch is a sleeping loft, where a guest can enjoy a good night's sleep with the whippoorwills."

PORCH WRAP

A small cabin can be a great interim structure on a piece of property meant ultimately for a more substantial retirement home. The cabin can later be used for guest quarters, a pool house, or a studio or office. With a modest investment, owners can begin enjoying their land on weekends, holidays, and summer vacations long before they intend to retire. It also allows them to more fully evaluate the property for the ideal site for their future home, experiencing it in all sorts of weather and throughout the year as the seasons change.

Kitty and Jim Delany found a spectacular parcel of land adjacent to a river half an hour from Chapel Hill, North Carolina. Although they live outside Chicago, the couple has a long history with the University of North Carolina and plans to retire to the area. With retirement at least a decade away, an interim structure seemed the most sensible approach to begin enjoying the property. The zoning laws allowed for a 1,000-sq.-ft. accessory building and they concluded that would suit them just fine.

The porch is oriented to the east, looking out over the spot where a swimming pool is planned. A porch sleeping loft provides rest in the fresh air.

First floor

Veranda

Bedroom

Living

Kitchen

Screened porch

Bedroom

Dining

Veranda

0　5　10

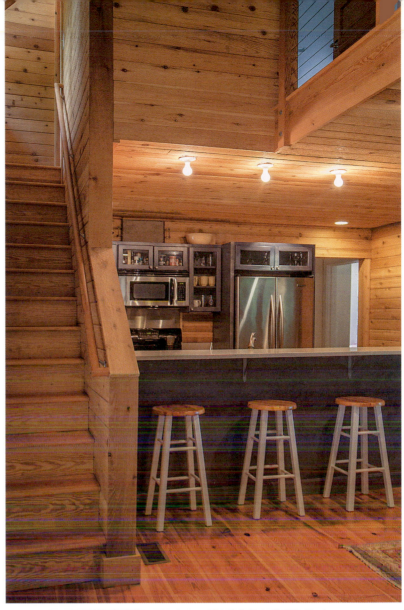

RIGHT This compact kitchen, tucked into a nook against the staircase, is a hub of activity. A raised counter hides the messiness of food prep from guests.

THE PORCH CABIN

There is a tradition in this country of cabins that are essentially little more than porches with a small enclosed interior space. A century ago it was a common for families (or the mother and children) to leave the city for the fresh air and sunshine of country living during the summer. There they would live in these sorts of porch cabins, cooking, eating, socializing, and sleeping in the open air. A single room with a fireplace was central to the plan, with porches surrounding it.

Area architect Georgia Bizios was hired to prepare a master plan for the property, one that would determine the best site for the interim structure (which would later be used as a guest cabin), their future retirement home, and a swimming pool, to be built at a later date. Her zoning interpretation noted that the 1,000-sq.-ft. limit was for tempered space (heated and air-conditioned), so a seasonal porch could be added on without being included in the limit.

The Delany property is a sloping hillside on the eastern bank of the river. A promontory was deemed the best location for the future home, with its panoramic views of the river. A plateau on a cooler forested northerly slope provided ample space for the interim/guest cabin and future swimming pool.

For the interim cabin, Bizios designed a broad-roofed structure housing two bedrooms, a bath, and social areas on one primary level. Its elongated floor plan allows for views to the east and north, as well as welcome cross-ventilation on steamy Carolina summer days.

Above this level is a multipurpose garret and below are a garage and storage space. The spacious screened porch is surrounded on both sides by open-air verandas, which provide more living space. High in the porch is a sleeping loft, where a guest can enjoy a good night's sleep with the whippoorwills, or a catnap while friends relax below.

OPPOSITE TOP The porch is a major component of the cabin, easily accommodating outdoor relaxation and dining. A rain chain channels the water down to the ground, reducing splashing into the porch.

OPPOSITE BOTTOM A second-level bridge connects indoor and outdoor living areas under the roof.

BELOW The architectural language of wood frames and metal railings creates an airy feeling and openness of spirit.

Second floor

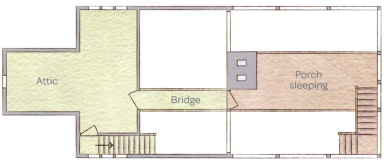

0   5   10

CREDITS

All photos by Cheryl Koralik, except as noted below.

GETTING AWAY FROM IT ALL
(PP. 2-9)
PHOTOS: Dale Mulfinger
ARCHITECT: Dale Mulfinger, FAIA,
SALA Architects, www.salaarc.com;
Gunter Dittmar

MEMORIES OF YESTERYEAR

LUNDIE'S LAGACY (PP. 12-19)
ARCHITECT: Edwin Lundie/Dale Mulfinger,
FAIA, SALA Architects

PARKS AND REC REDO (PP. 20-25)
ARCHITECT: Candace Tillotson-Miller, AIA,
Miller Architects; ctmarchitects.com

HER DREAM/HIS ENCHANTMENT
(PP. 26-31)
PHOTOS: Dale Mulfinger

BARN LIFE (PP. 32-37)
ARCHITECT: Candace Tillotson-Miller, AIA,
Miller Architects; ctmarchitects.com

ADIRONDACK CAMP (PP. 38-43)
ARCHITECT: Nils Luderowski, AIA;
www.luderowskiarchitect.com

BIRD'S EYE (PP. 44-49)
ARCHITECT: Lewis Butler, Butler Armsden
Architects; www.butlerarmsden.com

BACKYARD HIDEAWAY (PP. 50-55)
ARCHITECTS: Dale Mulfinger, FAIA, and
Chris Meyer, SALA Architects

ADD AND UPGRADE

SING ALONG (PP. 58-65)
ORIGINAL BUILDER: Edward Greenhalgh

ADDING CHARM (PP. 66-71)
architect/builder unknown

ACCESS TO WATER (PP. 72-77)
ARCHITECT: Jeremy Bonin, AIA, Bonin
Architects; www.boninarchitects.com

SIMPLE ELEGANCE (PP. 78-85)
ARCHITECT: Andy Ankeny, Carney Logan
Burke Architects; clbarchitects.com

"A" PLUS (PP. 86-91)
ARCHITECTS: John Rauma/Dale Mulfinger,
FAIA, SALA Architects

OLD GLORY (PP. 92-97)
BUILDER: Randy Gillen, Big Horn Custom
Builders; www.bighorncustombuild.com

SUBTRACT AND ADD (PP. 98-103)
ARCHITECT: Dale Mulfinger, FAIA,
SALA Architects

PREPACKAGED AND GIFT WRAPPED

INSTANT CABIN (PP. 106-111)
ARCHITECT: Geoffrey Warner, AIA,
Alchemy Architects; www.alchemyarch.com

GEORGIA PEACH (PP. 112-117)
ARCHITECT: Historical Concepts;
www.historicalconcepts.com

THE WELL-CONTAIN(ER)ED CABIN
(PP. 118-123)
ARCHITECTS: Paul Stankey and
Sarah Nordby

HOME RUN (PP. 124-129)
ARCHITECT: Ross Chapin, FAIA;
www.rosschapin.com

THE HAMLET (PP. 130-135)
BUILDER: Eric Mase, Wee Cabin Company;
www.weecabins.com

A KERNEL IDEA (PP. 136-141)
PHOTOS: Anice Hoachlander
ARCHITECT: Jeffery Broadhurst, AIA;
www.broadhurstarchitects.com

STEP LIGHTLY ON THE EARTH

STORY LINE (PP. 144-149)
BUILDER: Mark Johnson

ENERGY SHED (PP. 150-155)
ARCHITECT: David Arkin, AIA, Arkin Tilt
Architects; www.arkintilt.com

EARTH AND SKY (PP. 156-161)
PHOTOS: Dale Mulfinger
ARCHITECTS: Elizabeth and Winston Close;
www.closearchitects.com

CABIN CLASSROOM (PP. 162-167)
ARCHITECTS: Texas Tech University,
Urs Peter Flueckiger

THINKING LOCALLY (PP. 168-173)
PHOTOS: Dale Mulfinger
ARCHITECTS: Dale Mulfinger, FAIA, and
Carol O'Brien, SALA Architects

OPPOSITES ATTRACT (PP. 174-181)
ARCHITECT: E. Fay Jones

JUST FOR THE FUN OF IT

BASE CAMP FOR FUN (PP. 184-189)
ARCHITECTS: Dale Mulfinger, FAIA, and
Dan Wallace, SALA Architects

WE TOOK TO THE WOODS
(PP. 190-195)
ARCHITECT: Van Dam Architecture and
Design; www.vandamdesign.com;
SKETCH P. 193: Sam Van Dam

A WORK IN PROGRESS
(PP. 196-201)
BUILDER: Walter Johnson

ELFIN HEAVEN (PP. 202-209)
TIMBER FRAMER: Deane Hillbrand

BOARDING HOUSE (PP. 210-215)
ARCHITECTS: Dale Mulfinger, FAIA, and
Chris Meyer, SALA Architects
PHOTO TOP P. 215: Kathy Baker

LIGHT AND AIR

ONE BIG ROOM (PP. 218-223)
ARCHITECT: MaryAnn Thompson, AIA,
MaryAnn Thompson Architects;
www.maryannthompson.com

PANORAMIC VIEW (PP. 224-229)
PHOTOS: Dale Mulfinger
ARCHITECTS: Dale Mulfinger, FAIA, and
Chris Bubser, SALA Architects

LIGHT SHEDS (PP. 230-235)
PHOTOS: pp. 230, 233-235 Nic Lehoux;
p. 232 Andrew Latreille
SKETCH P. 235: Mark Osburn
ARCHITECTS: Andrew Latreille, Mark
Osburn, Osburn/Clarke Productions;
www.osburnclarke.com

SCREEN PLAY (PP. 236-241)
ARCHITECT: Henry Panton, Panton
Architect; www.pantonarchitect.com

PORCH WRAP (PP. 242-247)
ARCHITECT: Georgia Bizios, FAIA,
Bizios Architect; www.bizios.com

If you like this book, you'll love *Fine Homebuilding*.